HAUNTED HOTELS IN ARIZONA AND COLORADO

Ken Hudnall and Sharon Hudnall
OMEGA PRESS
EL PASO, TEXAS

HAUNTED HOTELS IN ARIZONA AND COLORADO
COPYRIGHT © 2016 KEN HUDNALL

All rights reserved. No part of this book may be reproduced or transmitted in any form or by any means, graphic, electronic, or mechanical, including photocopying, recording, taping or by any information storage or retrieval system, without the permission in writing from the publisher.

OMEGA PRESS

An imprint of Omega Communications Group, Inc.

For information contact:

Omega Press

5823 N. Mesa, #839

El Paso, Texas 79912

Or http://www.kenhudnall.com

FIRST EDITION

Printed in the United States of America

OTHER WORKS BY THE SAME AUTHOR FROM OMEGA PRESS

MANHATTAN CONSPIRACY SERIES
Blood on the Apple
Capitol Crimes
Angel of Death

THE OCCULT CONNECTION
UFOs, Secret Societies and Ancient Gods
The Hidden Race
Flying Saucers
UFOs and the Supernatural
UFOs and Secret Societies
UFOs and Ancient Gods
Evidence of Alien Contact
Secrets of Dulce
Intervention

SHADOW WARS
Shadow Rulers

DARKNESS
When Darkness Falls
Fear The Darkness

SPIRITS OF THE BORDER
(with Connie Wang)
The History and Mystery of El Paso Del Norte
The History and Mystery of Fort Bliss, Texas

(with Sharon Hudnall)
The History and Mystery of the Rio Grande
The history and Mystery of New Mexico

The History and Mystery of the Lone Star State
The History and Mystery of Arizona
The History and Mystery of Tombstone, AZ
The History and Mystery of Colorado
Echoes of the Past
El Paso: A City of Secrets
Tales From The Nightshift
The History and Mystery of Sin City
The History and Mystery of Concordia
Military Ghosts
Restless Spirits
School Spirits
Haunted Hotels
The History and Mystery of San Elizario, Texas

THE ESTATE SALE MURDERS
Dead Man's Diary

OTHER WORKS

Northwood Conspiracy

No Safe Haven; Homeland Insecurity

Where No Car Has Gone Before

Seventy Years and No Losses:

The History of the Sun Bowl

How Not To Get Published

Vampires, Werewolves and Things
That Go Bump In The Night

Even Paranoids Have Enemies

Criminal Law for Laymen

Understanding Business Law

Language of the Law

Border Escapades of Billy The Kid
PUBLISHED BY PAJA BOOKS
The Occult Connection: Unidentified Flying Objects

DEDICATION
As with all of my books, I could not have completed this book if not for my lovely wife, Sharon.

TABLE OF CONTENTS

ARIZONA   13
  ALPINE   13
    Hannagan Meadow Lodge   13
  BISBEE   15
    Old Bisbee Bed & Breakfast   15
    The Copper Queen Hotel   16
    The Inn At Castle Rock   20
    Oliver House   21
    OK STREET JAILHOUSE INN   23
    Clawson House Inn   24
    Bisbee Inn (Hotel La More)   25
  CHANDLER   27
    San Marcos Hotel   28
  DOUGLAS   29
    The Gadsden Hotel   30
  EL FRIDA   31
    Vision Quest Lodge   32
    Hotel Monte Vista   33
    Days Inn   35
    Northern Arizona University (NAU)   36
    North Morton Hall (NAU)   36
    Hotel Weatherford   37
  FLORENCE   39
    Arizona State Prison   40
  FORT HUACHUCA   41
    Carleton House   42
  GLOBE   49
    Globe High School   49
    Noftsger Hill Inn   49
  GRAND CANYON NATIONAL PARK   50
    El Tovar Hotel   50
  JEROME   51
    Connor Hotel   51

Jerome Grande Hotel	55
Ghost City Inn	58
The Palace – Haunted Hamburger	60
The Surgeon's House Bed and Breakfast	61
The Inn at Jerome	63
Jerome Inn and Grille Building	66
KINGMAN	71
Hotel Brunswick	71
NOGALES	73
Guevavi Mission	73
OATMAN	78
Oatman Hotel	78
ORACLE	81
Arcadia Ranch	81
PHOENIX	81
Arizona State Prison Complex - Flamenco Unit	81
Billington House	83
San Carlos Hotel	84
Tapatio Cliffs Resort- The Point Hilton	87
PRESCOTT	88
Hassayampa Inn	88
Hotel Vendome	91
Lynx Creek Farm Bed & Breakfast - Sharlot Hall	94
TOMBSTONE	95
Buford House	95
Victorian Garden's Bed and Breakfast	101
Tombstone Boarding House	103
Best Western Lookout Lodge	106
Maricopa Resident Hall	109
University of Arizona	109
TUCSON	114
Hotel Congress	114
Pioneer International Hotel	116
Radisson Hotel	119
WILLIAMS	120
Red Garter Bed and Bakery	120

YUMA	124
Hotel Lee	124
COLORADO	126
ALMA	126
The Schwartz Hotel	126
ASPEN	126
Hotel Jerome	127
BLACKHAWK	127
Gilpin Hotel & Casino	128
BOULDER	130
College Inn	131
Lumber Baron Inn -	132
CANON CITY	132
St. Cloud Hotel	133
CENTRAL CITY	134
Teller House	136
COLORADO SPRINGS	137
Black Forest Inn:	138
Broadmoor Hotel	138
Days Inn - Airport –	139
Cascade Blvd. - Hearthstone Inn –	139
Rock Ledge Ranch –	140
CRIPPLE CREEK	140
Imperial Hotel & Casino –	142
Palace Hotel & Casino –	142
DENVER	142
Brown Palace Hotel –	146
The Grosvenor Arms Apartments -	150
Hearthstone Inn -	155
Lumber Baron Inn:	160
Oxford Hotel:	168
Windsor Hotel	171
DURANGO	172
Strater Hotel	172
Jarvis Suites	173

The Rochester Hotel	173
EMPIRE	174
The Pratt Hotel	175
ESTES PARK	175
Baldpate Inn	176
The Stanley Hotel	177
EVERGREEN	181
Brook Forest Inn	182
FAIRPLAY	183
Fairplay Hotel	184
Hand Hotel	185
FLORENCE	186
Florence Hotel	186
FORT COLLINS	186
Helmshire Inn	187
Holiday Inn Holidome	187
GLENWOOD SPRINGS	188
Hotel Colorado	188
LEADVILLE	194
Alps Motel	197
Delaware Hotel	197
OURAY	201
Beaumont Hotel	203
Old Western Hotel	204
St. Elmo Hotel	205
REDSTONE	205
Redstone Inn	206
SILVERTON	208
Grand Imperial Hotel	208
STERLING	209
Ramada Inn	209
TRINIDAD	210
Tarabino Inn	211
YAMPA	218
The Royal Hotel -	218
INDEX	225

ARIZONA

ALPINE

Alpine, named for its altitude, is located in Apache County in the eastern part of the state. Alpine is at the eastern end of the White Mountains, in the Apache-Sitgreaves National Forest Former and merged names include: Bush Valley and Frisco.

Hannagan Meadow Lodge

The Hannagan Meadow Recreation Area is located in the White Mountains of eastern Arizona on US-191, the Coronado Highway. It is one of the most remote, unspoiled, and peaceful places in the state. The profound quietness is broken only by the occasional car on the road or the songbird. The nearest civilization is the hamlet of Alpine, 22 miles north. At 9,100 feet elevation, Hannagan Meadows offers cool summer weather and snow in the winter. Opportunities are excellent for summer hiking and winter cross-country skiing. There is trailhead access to the Blue Range Primitive Area, one of America's most remote and unspoiled wildernesses.

Since 1926, the historic Hannagan Meadow Lodge has provided rustic comfort in this beautiful and remote corner of Arizona's White Mountains. The lodge offers bed-and-breakfast rooms in its main building as well as ten rustic log cabins on the adjacent hillside. The rooms and cabins are well kept with high quality furnishings in authentic early Americana style. It is also occupied by the "Lady of the Lodge".

The ghostly occupant has been seen many times by those locking up for the night. As they lock the door and walk away, if they look back, many times they will see a light burning in the second floor hallway and a young woman in a white party dress will be seen standing in the second floor window. Of course, since there is no floor beneath the second floor window, anyone seen looking out it would have to be hovering in midair, but this does not stop the Lady of the Lodge. Many nights when staff members work late, the sound of mysterious footsteps are heard walking to the window where the lady is most often seen.

BISBEE

Bisbee, located 90 miles southeast of Tucson and nestled amongst the Mule Mountains, is the county seat of Cochise County. The community was founded in 1880 and named after Judge DeWitt Bisbee, a financial backer of the Copper Queen Mine. Once known as "the Queen of the Copper Camps", this Old West mining camp proved to be one of the richest mineral sites in the world, producing nearly three million ounces of gold and more than eight billion pounds of copper, not to mention the silver, lead and zinc that came from these rich Mule Mountains. By the early 1900s, the Bisbee Community was the largest city between St. Louis and San Francisco.

Old Bisbee Bed & Breakfast

The establishment known as the Old Bisbee Bed and Breakfast is located at 102 Tombstone Canyon Road. It has been reported that there is a presence in both the Blue Room

Figure 1: Old Bisbee Bed & Breakfast

and in Room 13, as well as in several other locations throughout the house.

In the Grandma Room various guests have reported what appeared to be an older woman watching over them during the night. Although the sightings reportedly made guests nervous, it was thought to be a benevolent spirit offering its presence as a protection.

The Copper Queen Hotel

Figure 2: the Copper Queen Hotel

The Copper Queen Hotel located at 11 Howell Avenue, was built in 1902 when Bisbee was still a booming mining camp. A tiny mining camp in 1877, Bisbee grew into a solid and wealthy town by 1910. The side canyon Brewery Gulch held more than 50 saloons in the early 1900s, earning a reputation as the best drinking and entertainment venue in the territory. Many of the fine commercial buildings and Victorian houses built in the boom years still stand. Many of these historic places have lingering spirits from the town's past within their walls.

The famous Copper Queen was built by the Copper Queen Mining Company[1] shortly after the turn of the century, when Bisbee was the largest mining town in the world. At the time this historic old hotel was constructed, Bisbee was a bustling metropolis with a population of over 20,000 with two opera houses and many permanent brick buildings.

The hotel played host to mining executives, traveling men, territorial governors and the flamboyant types of the Old West. The Arizona Territory was still a decade from statehood and Apache raiding parties were a menace to stagecoach travelers.

In keeping with his reputation for first class service, the Copper Queen Saloon was the gathering place for "officials and politicos". Just down the street from the "Queen" in what became known as "Brewery Gulch[2]," provided diversion for the miners with a number of bars and a vast number of shady ladies.

---

[1] The Copper Queen Mining Company later became the Phelps Dodge Corporation.
[2] Brewery Gulch was named after Muheim's Brewery.

Soon after Bisbee became a town, the Copper Queen Hotel came about as a place for dignitaries and weary miners to rest their hats.

Not unlike its rowdy neighbor, Tombstone, Bisbee's character and legend can be traced back to Western vigilantes, rowdy saloons, brawling miners, gunfights and a colorful cast of characters people are still talking about.

Bisbee made its fortune from copper throughout the 1920s and even hung on through the 1970s when the mines closed down.

In keeping with its history, there is no doubt among many that I have talked to that the Copper Queen Hotel is also host to an array of ghosts. A number of visitors to this historic old hotel talk about a dark figureless apparition that has been seen wandering the halls of the 3rd floor. It is believed that this apparition is the spirit of young woman who died at the Copper Queen Hotel. She has appeared in both the Café and in Room 318. As if this is not enough to whet the appetite of the most intrepid ghost hunter, I have also been told that the unusual occurrences are not just limited to room 318 and the Café.

Former employees have reported that on occasion the elevator will stop between floors and staff members who come to help any quests trapped inside the elevator report that they can hear people inside the elevator carrying on conversations. However when the elevator is entered, it is discovered that there is no one inside.

In Room 210 I have been told of guests hearing the sound of someone stomping around in heavy boots. Toothpaste has also been seen to shoot across the room. Others have reported the sounds of a lady singing and the lights have been known to flicker on and off.

Though there are reported incidents throughout the hotel, it appears as if the 3rd floor is the most active part of the hotel. Guests and staff have reported doors opening and closing by themselves and electrical appliances operating on their own accord. Cold spots in the rooms and hallways often accompany this activity.

In Room 303 it has been reported that furniture has been moved and the odor of cigar smoke is often detected in the room. Guests in Room 304 have reported that late at night they have heard the sound of the doorknob to the room jiggling as if someone is trying to enter. The doorknob is also said to lock by itself. In Room 308 there have been reports of the door to the bathroom opening and closing by itself. In Room 312 it has been reported that an apparition is seen who is said to be named "Billy".

Room 315 is inhabited by a most unusual female ghost. It is believed that she is the spirit of Miss Julia Lowell, a prostitute who made the Copper Queen her home for many years. It is not unusual for Julia to favor those men she likes with her attentions. Some have awakened to hear her whispering in their ear. She has been seen, in a very real sense on the staircase and to a very lucky few, she has appeared as she was in life, performing a very erotic dance in the room. When those so favored reach for her, she smiles and fades away.

In Room 412 it has been reported that the windows open and close by themselves. There have also been reported of both guests as well as staff members seeing the apparition of a little boy crying on this floor. When approached, however, the little boy is said to fade away.

The Inn At Castle Rock

Figure 3: The sign welcoming customers.

It is said that an artesian spring once flowed at the base of the famous Castle Rock. In 1877, an army sergeant stopping for water found traces of silver in this hidden alcove and so began a small silver rush. Unfortunately, overzealous miners dug into the spring and flooded the mine. The spring[3] was capped off and made into the town well.

In 1895, Joseph Muirhead, Bisbee's first mayor, built a boarding house on this spot for miners. The building was converted into apartments and then into a bed and breakfast in 1982. The owner of the bed and breakfast was Jim Babcock and it is now thought that he is one of the ghosts that haunt the building.

Each of the rooms is named and in one, called the Tasmania Room, many guests and visitors report experiencing the feeling of being watched.

Oliver House

The Oliver House is a historic home that is now an inviting twelve room bed and breakfast located at 26 Souls Street, deep in the Historic District. This historical home in Bisbee, the Oliver house is haunted by several spirits. Edith Oliver built the house for executives of the various mining companies until they all merged in the Dodge Phillips Corporation.

---

[3] The spring was christened Apache Spring.

The house has also served as a boarding house for miners. In keeping with the rough and ready lifestyle of these early residents, it is said that twenty seven people have died in the home since its construction. The house is also the scene of an unsolved murder.

In the late 1800's, Nathan Anderson, a resident of this rooming house was found shot between the eyes in the room at the top of the staircase. He was with a woman, who was also dead of a gunshot wound. It is rumored that Anderson was bedding the wife of a local policeman who, upon discovering the affair stalked them until he caught them in bed together. When he discovered them, the wronged husband shot them both before heading downstairs to kill everyone who happened to be in the parlor. He was then said to have driven to the edge of town and committed suicide.

It is also rumored that there another murder committed in this house, but the culprit was never found. In spite of these tragic occurrences and the hauntings that have resulted, overall, it is said that the building is pleasant and very nostalgic.

Guests that have stayed in the murder room have heard what they thought were firecrackers exploding in the hall. Later they reported hearing the opening and slamming of doors with heavy footsteps going down the hall. They found out in the morning that no one else had heard any of the sounds they did, but that previous guests had reported similar events.

There is another room called the Grandma room in which an older lady died of natural causes. It has been reported that she stays in the residence as a kind of protector. She moves the rocking chair and prefers to rock in front of the window. She is seen late at night in the room, either in the rocking chair or dusting the room.

People staying in the Purple Sage room have witnessed the shutters and doors opening and closing by themselves. The Plum room has moving cold spots and people have the feeling of being watched.

OK STREET JAILHOUSE INN

Figure 4: The Jailhouse Inn

This Inn was originally built in 1904 as a branch of the Cochise County Jail. Located just one block from the famous Brewery Gulch, it was very convenient for the local law officers to haul those who misbehaved to jail. However, by 1915, the two story jail was unable to handle all of those who needed a place to sleep it off. To alleviate the overcrowding, a large detention facility was built and the jailhouse was abandoned to sit empty for many years.

During the 1950s, Bisbee was often used as a favorite location for the filming of westerns. John Wayne became part owner of the Jailhouse which was used as temporary living quarters. Then in 1988, the jailhouse was converted into a two level suite and it has been a guest house ever since.

Guests have reported feeling watched as they sat in their rooms reading or otherwise amusing themselves. A number of photos have shown what seem to be orbs floating near the barred windows as if watching the world from their cells.

Clawson House Inn
116 Clawson Avenue

The Clawson House Inn is a 3 room Bed and Breakfast that has long catered to miners. In the 1890's there were several labor disputes between the miners and the mine owners. One of the most violent was between the owners of the Queen Mine and the miners. Unwilling to compromise, the mine owners had large numbers of the dissatisfied miners rounded up and shipped out of the area. Strikebreakers were brought in to claim the jobs left vacant by the strike.

Three of the strikebreakers rented rooms at the Clawson House. It is said that they were killed by the strikers and now haunt the house along with the spirit of Mrs. Clawson, herself.

Bisbee Inn (Hotel La More)

Figure 5: Bisbee Inn

The history of Hotel La More/The Bisbee Inn predates its actual construction. Acquired from Mexico in 1853 as part of the Gadsden Purchase, Lots 11 and 12, Block One, of the Bisbee town site were deeded to the City of Bisbee by the U.S. Government in 1904 and purchased by J.P. Hill in 1905. Early photographs of this site on Chihuahua Hill show two wooden buildings, described in directories of the time as housing "rooms" and "furnished rooms."

As Bisbee prospered and grew, the dirt track leading along the lower slope of Chihuahua Hill, originally called "OK Trail," became OK Street. Lots 11 and 12 were sold to Mrs. S.P. Bedford who, in 1916, constructed a substantial, 24-room hotel building on the site of the wooden buildings which had been destroyed by fire.

Mrs. Bedford furnished the hotel and leased it to Mrs. Kate La More on October 1, 1917, for $160 per month. The 1917 Bisbee directory lists the "Hotel La More" as "just up the hill from the depot," with rates of $2 per day or $8 per week. The hotel was advertised as "the most modern in Bisbee."

The Bisbee Inn has changed its name back to the Hotel La More. Located in Brewery Gulch, it was a favorite haven for the shady ladies of Bisbee. Now it is said to be a favorite haunt of some spirits.

The activity is not centered around a particular section of the hotel. Beds are torn apart and the outline of an invisible person lying on the beds is visible at times. Chairs and tables are moved about in the hallways.

"Abigail" appears as a foggy tornado between the bed and door of several upstairs rooms. Another ghost is rumored to be Michele, a blond prostitute, who haunts the first floor. The Spirits here do not like people and activity drops when the hotel is busy. Generally, the spirits here do not show themselves to the employees, only the guests.

CHANDLER

In 1891, Dr. Alexander John Chandler, the first veterinary surgeon in Arizona Territory, settled on a ranch south of Mesa, studying irrigation engineering. By 1900, he had acquired 18,000 acres of land, and began drawing up plans for a town site on what was then known as the Chandler Ranch. The town site office opened on May 17, 1912, the same year that Chandler High School was established. By 1913, a town center had become established, featuring the luxurious Hotel San Marcos, the first golf resort in the state.

While Chandler stagnated through the Great Depression, the founding of Williams Air Force Base in 1941 led to a small surge in population, but Chandler still only held 3,800 people by 1950. By 1980, it had grown to 30,000, and it has since paced the Phoenix metropolitan area's high rate of growth, with vast suburban residential areas swallowing former agricultural plots. Some of this growth was fueled by the establishment of manufacturing plants for communications and computing firms such as Motorola and Intel, but despite the inclusion of many large businesses, Chandler is often considered a bedroom community for the greater Phoenix metropolitan area.

San Marcos Hotel

Figure 6: San Marcos Hotel

The San Marcos Hotel, located at 1 San Marcos Place is a beautiful hotel that has a darker side. Staff members, who have manned the reception desk at night, report receiving strange calls from extensions that don't exist. Attempts to trace these calls always end in failure.

Both guests and staff have reported seeing a female apparition moving through the hotel and some have even reported hearing the moaning of a male. To date there have been no reports of the male being seen, but he has certainly been heard.

DOUGLAS

Douglas is a city in Cochise County, Arizona (USA). It is named after mining pioneer James Douglas. The population was 14,312 at the 2000 census. Douglas stands on the U.S.-Mexico border, across from the city of Agua Prieta, Sonora, (Mexico).

Douglas was also the site of the Phelps-Dodge Corporation Douglas Reduction Works until its closure in 1987. Two copper smelters operated at the site. The Calumet and Arizona Company Smelter was built in 1902. The Copper Queen operated in Douglas from 1904 until 1931, when the Phelps-Dodge Corporation purchased the Calumet and Arizona Company and took over their smelter. The Calumet and Arizona smelter then became the Douglas Reduction Works.

The Gadsden Hotel

Figure 7: Gadsden Hotel

The Gadsden Hotel is located at 1046 G. Avenue and opened its doors in 1907. Named for the Gadsden Purchase, the stately five-story, 160-room hotel became a home away from home for cattlemen, ranchers, miners, and businessmen in the young Arizona territory. The hotel was leveled by fire and rebuilt in 1929. The Gadsden is recognized as a National Historic Site.

The Gadsden's spacious main lobby is majestically set with a solid white Italian marble staircase and four soaring marble columns. An authentic Tiffany stained glass mural extends forty-two feet across one wall of the massive mezzanine. An impressive oil painting by Audrey Jean Nichols is just below the Tiffany window. Vaulted stained glass skylights run the full length of the lobby.

There have been reports of a headless figure floating through the halls. This figure has been seen many times in the basement of the old building. There are many who believe that this is the spirit of Pancho Villa. Oddly enough, it is also said that this figure generally appears during Lent.

There is another figure that may well be the same one seen floating about the halls, that is said to ride up the marble stairs on a ghostly horse. This figure is also dressed in khaki military style clothing.

The hotel was restored in 1988 to its former appearance and this really seemed to stir up the spirits. Almost all of the staff and many guests have come in contact with one or more of the spirits that seem to call the Gadsden their home. There is the Indian Boy that likes to play on the Mezzanine level, who is known to be a real prankster. Then there is the elderly lady, known as Sara, who likes to spend her time on the 4th floor.

EL FRIDA

El Frida is an unincorporated community in Cochise County.

Vision Quest Lodge

Vision Quest Learning Center is located at 2491 Jefferson Road on what was formerly a dude ranch. According to reports, while it was a dude ranch, a stable boy went insane and killed owners and guests. There are reports that a woman in white gown haunts the old guest quarters. Others say that the house where owners were killed has several weird events that take place there. According to reports a woman walks halls and there is a re-occurring bloodstain on the bathroom wall.

Inside the Old Stable a number of people report have seen a two-year-old child being killed by a horse kicking her. The sounds of a child's crying and the apparition of a child standing in the doorway of the stable are common. Also, the apparition of white glowing man on a white glowing horse has been seen in mountains that border the camp.

Hotel Monte Vista
100 N. San Francisco Street
Flagstaff AZ

Figure 8: Hotel Monte Vista

The Hotel Monte Vista is a large hotel that opened in 1927 and was the home base to many actors when Westerns were popular and often filmed near Flagstaff. Hence many rooms are named after 1940's era actors. While enjoying a drink in the cocktail lounge in this hotel, many have reported sensing the spirit of the bank robber who died of his gunshot wounds in that section of the building. Ironically, he was enjoying a drink himself at the time of his collapse, celebrating his successful heist.

According to the story, three thieves planned on robbing the nearby bank. They agreed that if they were successful that they would celebrate their success by having a drink in the bar of the Hotel Monte Vista. They were successful, but one of the thieves was wounded. He made it as far as the hotel bar where he died enjoying his last drink.

No one seems to know why, but many say that there is the ghost of a former bellboy that haunts Room 210, also known as the Zane Grey[4] Suite. Many have reported that he often knocks on the door and announces that room service has arrived. When the startled guest opens the door, the hall is empty. An image of a woman has also been seen outside the Zane Grey Room and sounds of a man coughing continuously all night long have been heard.

A number of guests have experienced some strange things in Room 220, as did the maintenance man who returned to the room five minutes after leaving and locking it up only to find the TV on at full blast and the bed linens stripped.

In room 305, guests have complained of a rocking chair that continues to rock though empty. The chair is also reported to move to different parts of the room, through each time it is in a position to look out the window.

There has also been a story told of a lady seeing a man trying to enter room 309. Finally, when his key seemed not to work, he walked through the solid door and vanished. The witness stated that the man looked like the actor Alan Ladd. Room 309 is the Alan Ladd suite.

---

[4] Zane Grey donated half of the necessary funds to build the hotel. The balance was raised through public subscription.

John Wayne also had a suite named after him, Room 402. He once told the story of entering the room and seeing a ghost standing near a table.

In the Gary Cooper Room a guest was unnerved by the distinct feeling that someone was staring at him. It turns out that two prostitutes had been murdered in that room.

There are also stories told about the basement of the hotel. A number of staff members have heard the sounds of a baby crying though numerous searches have failed to find any sign of anyone in the basement.

Days Inn

Figure 9: Days Inns

From the Days Inn at 3601 E. Lockett Rd come reports that guests have awoken from a sound sleep to see the ghost of a tall man standing next to the bed looking down at them. If they react to his presence, it is said that he will fade away. No one seems to have any idea who this figure might be.

Northern Arizona University (NAU)

Northern Arizona Normal School (NANS) opened its doors on September 11, 1899 with twenty-three students, one professor, and two copies of Webster's International Dictionary bound in sheepskin. The Normal School's first president, Almon Nicholas Taylor, later assisted by Ms. Frances Bury, had scoured the countryside in horse and buggy seeking students to fill the classrooms of the single school building, now known as Old Main. From the students they recruited, four women made up the first graduating class of 1901 and received lifetime teaching certificates for the Arizona Territory.

North Morton Hall (NAU)

Figure 10: Morton Hall

North Morton Hall is certainly one of the most notorious haunted locations in Flagstaff. According to legend, a girl killed herself in the dormitory many years ago, shortly before the Christmas break and it would appear that she never left.

There have been reports of lights going on and off, unexplained odors, and even sightings of this lonely ghost. There have also been reports that she likes to pull blankets off of people that stay on the floor she lived on, and she likes to trap girls in the girls' bathroom. A number of the victims of her pranks report that once they enter the bathroom, it appears that the door is locks behind them, but there isn't a lock.

Hotel Weatherford

Figure 11: Hotel Weatherford

When Arizona was just a territory and vigilantes ruled the dusty streets and trails, in rode John W. Weatherford to Flagstaff. Having a grand vision for Flagstaff, Weatherford soon began to build what would become known as one of the finest hotels in the West. Opening on New Year's Day, 1900, the luxurious hotel would attract such visitors as newspaper tycoon, William Randolph Hearst, former President Theodore Roosevelt, and Old West author, Zane Grey, and lawman, Wyatt Earp. After his luxury hotel was complete, John Weatherford built the Majestic Opera House, which opened in 1911. When it burned down in 1915, Weatherford was not to be deterred and rebuilt his theater, this time calling it the Orpheum, which continues to stand today.

In the early part of the 20th century, watercolor artist Thomas Moran spent many nights at the Weatherford Hotel while he completed his sketches of western landscapes. These works of art were partially responsible for moving Congress to preserve such places as the Grand Canyon and Yellowstone as National Parks.

Over the years this historic building served a number of purposes, include Flagstaff's first telephone exchange company, a number of restaurants, a theater, a radio station and a billiard hall. Today, it has been fully restored and again caters to Flagstaff travelers

Along with its rich history, the Hotel Weatherford is also said to be called home to a couple of resident ghosts. The Zane Grey Ballroom, complete with its stained glass windows and antique Brunswick bar moved from Tombstone, is said to be the site where at least one of Weatherford's ghosts is said to most often appear. In this beautiful ballroom the ghostly woman has often been spied floating across the room. On other occasions, she is said to dart from one side of the room to the other. Other phenomenon in the ballroom includes the light over the pool table that seemingly sways of its own accord and the sounds of whispers and voices coming from an otherwise empty bar.

Apparently, there the ghosts of a long ago bride and groom also haunt the hotel. According to the legend, the honeymoon couple was murdered in Room 54 of the hotel back in the 1930s. On at least one occasion, an employee who was staying in the hotel, awoke in the middle of the night to find a bride and groom sitting on the foot of the bed. Today, the room has been turned into a storage closet, but that hasn't stopped the ghostly pair, as guests have often reported seeing the couple enter the room. Staff often report hearing their names being called out by an unseen spirit while on the fourth floor as well as feeling a presence standing behind them.

FLORENCE

Florence is a town in Pinal County, Arizona, United States. The population was 17,054 at the 2000 census. The city is the county seat of Pinal CountyGR6. The largest Arizona State Prison complex is located in the city, and its preserved Main Street and open desert scenery was the setting of the major motion picture "Murphy's Romance".

Arizona State Prison

Figure 12: Arizona State Prison

In Florence, Arizona State Prison's Cellblock 3 and the death house are said to be haunted by those incarcerated or guarding prisoners. During a riot in 1973, two officers, named Buckely and Morey, were beaten and stabbed to death in this cellblock by inmates. On several occasions when guards had locked all of the doors in the cellblock, they would find doors open in between inmate counts. Officers also have felt cold spots and heard the sounds of doors opening and closing as well as seeing misty forms appearing, according to "Haunted Hotspots in Arizona." The cellblock is located in the same location as the Arizona death house, which is said to be haunted by the ghosts of condemned prisoners. The house contains a gas chamber and lethal injection room. Guards have reported hearing screams and other strange sounds, "Haunted Hotspots" says.

ASP Cellblock 3 is located in the same location as the Arizona Death House, which also house a gas chamber and a lethal injection chamber. Both of these are said to also be haunted. It is said that the ghosts of condemned prisoners haunt the death house at the state prison in Florence. Several guards have reported hearing screams and other strange sounds.

FORT HUACHUCA

Fort Huachuca, Arizona was built around 1877 and played an important role during the Indian wars of the 1870's and 1880's. It served as the advance headquarters and the supply base in the campaign against Geronimo. Later the Tenth Cavalry was headquartered here during General John Pershing's 1916 campaign into Mexico to find Pancho Villa. The fort was also home to four regiments of "Buffalo Soldiers", the African-American army units of the late 1800's and early 1900's. In 1954, the fort became the site for advanced testing of electronics and communications equipment and today is the Army Intelligence Center and School and the Army's Information Systems Command. All C130 flight training for NATO takes place at the fort, as does some training for the Israeli air force and army. But despite all of this advance technology and training, some elements of the fort's past continue to linger on as hauntings!

Carleton House

Carleton House is the oldest building on the base. It was originally constructed as the post hospital back in 1880 and was named for Brig. General James H. Carleton, the famous leader of the "California Column" during the Civil War. It remained a hospital for a few years and then was turned into housing quarters for officers, an officer's mess, post headquarters, a cafe, and then a schoolhouse. Between 1947 and 1951, when the fort was briefly given back to the state of Arizona, Carleton House was used as a vacation retreat by Governors Sidney P. Osborn and Dan E. Garvey. In more recent years, is has been the residence of the hospital commander or other officers assigned to the base.

Perhaps the most famous of those who have encountered the ghost of the Carleton House has been Colonel Roy Strom, who was the deputy commander of the U.S. Army Intelligence Center from 1980-1982. Even today, he refers to the house as being "haunted". Prior to he and his family's residency though, a number of families had reported odd happenings in the house. His wife, Joan

Strom, would eventually attach a name to the ghost and call her "Charlotte".

When the Strom's first moved into the house, the reputation of the place was made quickly evident to them when one of the moving crew became jittery and refused to go into the place. His fellow workers were upset with what seem to be nothing but laziness. "I'm not going in there," he told them. "That house is haunted."

One downstairs room was the original morgue for the hospital. Things stacked and placed in this room are unaccountably scattered all over the place shortly afterwards. Things hanging on the walls fall to the floor because the nails holding them are pulled out of the wall by an invisible force.

Not knowing about this activity, on that same day, the Strom's piled boxes in what had been the hospital's morgue. Later that night, they discovered the boxes had been pulled open and the contents strewn about. And this wasn't the last of it! A few days later, the doorbell began to ring over and over again. Each time they would check to see who the visitor was, they would find no one there. Colonel Strom guessed it to be kids pulling a prank and so the next time it rang, he ran around the side of the house to catch the culprits. There was no one there! He eventually disconnected the wiring to the bell.

The family also experienced lights turning on an off, erratic electrical problems, wall hangings that moved and refused to stay straight and one particular place in the house that was very cold. In this one corner of the living room, the air was drastically colder than the rest of the house and the overhead light above it refused to work properly. Joan Strom dubbed this "Charlotte's Corner".

Joan believed that the ghost was that of a woman from the frontier period who had died in the fort's hospital during the early 1880's. While she lived in the house, she searched fort records and a cemetery trying to find evidence of her death, but without success. Her searching paid off in other ways though when she got a glimpse of what she believed was Charlotte's ghost! One morning, Joan thought she saw her teen-aged daughter Amy walk down an adjacent hallway from the kitchen. Amy never stopped or returned the greeting that Joan called out to her. Thinking this was unusual, she went to Amy's room to check on her. Here, she found Amy fast asleep and when she checked her other daughter's rooms, she found that they too were asleep and had not been in the hallway.

But Joan's sighting is an oddity in the haunted history of the house. Although the place has been reportedly haunted for years, sightings of the ghost are rare. One of the first sightings occurred to a neighbor who came to deliver a message to the Koenig's, residents of the house before the Strom family. The boy didn't know that the house's front door was actually located on the side, so he went up the front steps and knocked. He later told his parents that Margaret Koenig walked right down the hall toward him but ignored his knocking. She had blond hair and wore a dressing gown. Bothered by this, the boy's mother later telephoned Mrs. Koenig, who insisted that she and her family had just arrived home and that no one had been in the house at the time of the boy's call!

Nancy Koenig, one of Margaret's daughters, also claimed to see the ghost. She was returning late from a date one night and as promised, went to let her mother know that she had made it home all right. When she spotted her mother standing in the hallway, she called out to her and then went to bed. The following morning, Margaret scolded the girl for not letting her know that she was home but Nancy protested and described the woman that she had seen. Strangely though, Margaret was never in the hallway and had been asleep when Nancy had come in!

Many residents and neighbors have seen the whitish apparition of a woman moving through the house and standing at the front door. One corner of a room, which was a ward in the original hospital, stays markedly colder than all other parts of the house, regardless of the weather, and contains a chandelier that seems to refuse to operate at night but functions just fine in the daylight.

Other manifestations include:

- A daughter's jewelry box mysteriously flew off the fireplace in her room, and landed in the middle of the room's rug.

- After a struggle, one family was able to securely hang pictures in the knotty pine paneled living room, which was the hospital's ward for patients. The next morning, they found all their pictures on the floor. A solid brass, Asian trivet that was also hung on the wall, was bent nearly in half, and was impossible to bend back into position by hand. It seems someone didn't approve of their taste in decorations, and perhaps resented the invasion of her space.

- In the living room, the four chandeliers experienced unexplainable electrical problems.

- The one chandelier that is located over a part of the living room that is always colder than the rest of the house, never would work in the evening hours. Mrs. S made this colder part of the living room, Charlotte's corner. Another resident family, later put a rocking chair and a doll in it to perhaps comfort the ghost, and let her know she has her own space there to rest, if searching for her child gets to be too frustrating. Perhaps this is the area in the then hospital ward that she died giving birth.

Charlotte has made appearances to various members of several families, and the neighbors as well.

- One boy, who had fallen asleep in the TV room, awoke and had to go through the paneled living room, past Charlotte's corner in order to get to his bedroom, the one mentioned above as being the old hospital morgue. As he past Charlotte's corner, he saw a long dress standing by itself, with no one seen inside it. It was an 1880's dress, often worn by young women in Arizona at this time. The light colored dress was a gown with ruffled edges around the sleeves and hem line.

- A young woman, mistaken for Mrs. S's daughter, was seen walking down the hallway near the kitchen. It wasn't the daughter, as thought by her mother, as the daughter was sleeping in bed at the time of this sighting.

- While Mrs. S was carrying her clean towels to the linen closet, a white mist swirled all around her, engulfing her. It wasn't cold, damp, threatening or frightening, just eerie.

- A neighbor boy had run to the house to deliver a message when no one was home. He saw a blond-haired young woman in a dressing gown walking down the hallway, who ignored his door knocks.

- Mrs. K's daughter had agreed to check in with her mother after she came in from a date that night. When the daughter got home that evening, she went into the paneled living room and saw a woman standing at the end of the hall. She said goodnight to who she thought was her mom. The next morning, her mom asked her why she didn't check in with her as agreed to, and then learned that her daughter had said goodnight to the apparition instead.

Mr. and Mrs. T have heard voices.

- In the wee hours of the morning, Mr. T was in the kitchen, studying for an exam, and the door was shut to the dining room. He heard a young voice call to him from just the other side of this door, saying "Daddy, Daddy!" No one was there, and his son was fast asleep.

- Mrs. T was standing out on the porch in the early morning, around 5 AM. She heard a mechanical sounding voice coming from the house saying, "Sleep, sleep!"

For sensitive people, the little cellar room gives the living a sense of dread and uneasiness upon entering it. Mr. T came in to investigate the non-working water heater, but had to leave quickly as he was suddenly awash with dread. Psychics believe that somewhere in this room, Charlotte's baby was buried in an unmarked spot.

GLOBE

Globe High School

There are a number of stories told about Globe High School about creaking floor boards and disembodied voices being heard in this school. There is also a haunted bathroom where one particular toilet would violently shake when anyone tried to use it. There were also a number of stories of ghosts on the top floor as well.

Noftsger Hill Inn

Figure 13: Noftsger Hill Inn

The Noftsger Hill Inn sits atop a hill outside overlooking Globe. It was built in 1907 as the North Globe Schoolhouse. In 1917, the building was enlarged and the name changed to the Noftsger Hill School[5]. The school served the children of Globe until 1981 when it was closed.

According to the locals, a lantern light could be seen at night and children were hearing voices and objects such as books were moved. After the school was closed, the

---

[5] The school was named after Globe businessman A. N. Noftsger.

property was bought and re-opened as a bed and breakfast. Since that time, guests have reported hearing the sounds of children laughing and talking and the figure of an older white haired man has been seen in one of the room.

GRAND CANYON NATIONAL PARK

El Tovar Hotel

Figure 14: El Tovar Hotel

Although most visitors are not aware of this, the El Tovar Hotel is home to several spirits. In the middle of the U shaped parking lot in front of the El Tovar Hotel, there is a marked grave hiding in a patch of land next to the stop sign. The grave is that of a former Harvey Girl that worked for Fred Harvey Company. The ghost of a black caped figure has been seen walking along the pathway leading up from the steps just to the right of the El Tovar Hotel all along the path, passing the grave and disappearing behind the Hopi House. Although most visitors are unaware, the El Tovar, built in the very early 1900's, is home to more than a few spirits. They say that Fred Harvey appears on the third floor during the holidays and invites people to the annual Christmas gathering held in the hotel. The third floor and the kitchen are the haunted hot spots at the El Tovar Hotel.

JEROME

As one walks down the streets of Jerome you can almost feel the ghosts of the past in the air. In fact, the town is affectionately known as "The Ghost City". The city has many residents from bygone eras that refuse to leave. Locals call their community center "spook hall" because of the ghost of a prostitute sighted there.

The white misty figure of an unidentified phantom has been spotted at the Old Episcopal Church (located halfway up Cleopatra Hill) and ghosts abound at the "Old Company Clinic" (now a deserted building just below the present hospital), including the spectral re-enactment of a terrible influenza epidemic that devastated the town back in 1917.

Connor Hotel

The Connor Hotel was built by David Connor in 1898. Though the historic old hotel has burned down twice, it has been rebuilt each time.

Figure 15: The Connor Hotel

The original structure built by David Connor on this location was a one story building called the Stone Saloon. However, as demand grew, he expanded it to the two story structure that it is today.

Some of the spirits encountered at various times here include a woman in Room 1 who whispers in the ears of guests as they sleep. Those who hear the whispering ghost also report feeling an icy cold in the room. An artist who stayed in Room 1 kept seeing a Lady in Red in his dreams. He painted the large mural found above the bar in the Spirit Room, including a picture of this Lady in Red.

In Room 2, the dog of one of the desk clerks encountered something that terrified the dog. It was also reported that the desk chair will not stay pushed beneath the desk. It is always moved close to the window.

In Room 3, guests have reported encountering a slim gray haired man who is normally seen near the bathroom door.

In Room 5, electronic items will not function properly. The satellite television will not function properly and the laptops and cell phones of guests will refuse to function. Guests in other nearby rooms have also complained about the dog inside Room 5 growling throughout the night even when the room is empty. People staying in Room 5 have experienced both hot and cold spots, having the hair on their arms and neck stand straight up, and heard strange noises as well. Entities in general are fascinated with electrical gadgets and can't help but play with them! When Room 5 is empty, the alarm clock has been known to go off by itself, not been set by the living but a ghost getting some chuckles.

In Room 9, which has had very few reports of strange occurrences, a guest came out of the bathroom and saw a small man in a dark suite and bowler hat sitting on the bed beside her husband who was lying down at the time. When she called to her husband to look at their visitor, the little man vanished.

The 2nd Floor Bathroom has also been the scene of several events. A relative of the current owner was using the bathroom facilities in the second floor bathroom, when she heard a very soft but clear man's voice calling her, not once but twice, encouraging a hasty retreat downstairs. She thought she was alone on the 2nd floor. She was except for a friendly Male Spirit!

Spirit Photographers, as they photographed the stairs, hallway and rooms, felt they were being followed by an unseen entity. When they developed their pictures, they captured "the vortex of an Invisible Entity on the stairs."

Other stories have included the spirit of a young girl in the lobby and that of a man who climbs the stairs but never makes it to the top floor. One final story involves a couple and their dog that stayed at the hotel. They asked the woman at the front desk if there where ghosts they needed to know about and she just shrugged and said "If you have an open mind you'll have an experience." They experienced sudden drops in temperature, the coffee pot turning off, the dog being scared of something on the wall, and all of the batteries in their electronic items being drained of power.

In the past, the Lady in Red has appeared to unsuspecting people who were alone in the bar or in other parts of the building. She is reported to just stand there, looking at the person, and then slowly fades away. In the past, people have reported that they were touched by an unseen entity in the bar and other places in the building. People have reported having "odd, strange feelings," in the bar and other parts of the building.

In the first floor shops there have been several events. Two ghosts, a man and a woman, like to wander through the artesian shops, to keep an eye on the living, "help out" and get some chuckles and attention at the expense of the living. Perhaps these two ghosts are the ones who make their home base on the 2nd floor in The Connor Hotel of Jerome.

Jerome Grande Hotel

Figure 16: The Jerome Grande Hotel

The Jerome Grande Hotel is housed in a Spanish Mission style building, constructed in 1926, that started out as the United Verde Hospital, opening January, 1927. In 1930, it was written up as the most modern and well equipped hospital in Arizona and possibly the Western States. The Hospital was closed in 1950 as the mine operation was being phased out. The building stood unused for the next 44 years until the rehabilitation plans started in 1994.

Probably the best known ghost in the Jerome Grande Hotel is that of a former maintenance man by the name of Claude Harvey. Mr. Harvey is said to have died in April of 1935 when his head was pinned underneath the elevator which he had been trying to repair. There were no witnesses to this unexplained death and it was chalked up to an accident. However, it may well have been murder as the only way that this death could have happened in this fashion was if someone had bypassed the safety switch.

The ghost of Mr. Harvey is said to still roam the hotel. The shadowy figure of a man is often seen loitering about the hallways and orbs of light are often seen inside the elevator shaft. Often the sounds of the elevator moving are heard even though the elevator is parked on the top floor and not in service.

One staff member is said to have had an encounter with a ghostly cat that likes to jump onto her bed. This same staff member has felt a presence behind her often and on more than one occasion, she has felt something invisible touch her arm.

One night, a desk clerk heard the sounds of someone moving about the gift shop as well as the sounds of items being dropped on the floor. When she investigated, it was found that the shop was empty, but a number of smaller items had been knocked to the floor from some of the shelves.

In one of the second floor rooms, a guest saw a woman's face peering through the window from the outside. The smells of cigarette smoke as well as that of whiskey have also been detected at certain times. Another guest, staying in a room on the third floor reported the strong odor of ether in her room. The operating rooms of the old hospital were on the third floor and ether was used as an anesthetic. There have also been reports of guests hearing voices and loud conversations coming from empty rooms, including rooms 31, 33, 39A and 39B.

There have been a number of reports of strange things on the fourth floor as well. One guest reported seeing a man's face staring at her from her bathroom mirror. Another reported seeing floating lights moving up and down the hallway.

As if these occurrences are not enough, there have also been reports of footsteps moving about the hallways during the night and what sounds like the squeaking of wheels of things being rolled down the halls when the hallways are empty. Doors open and shut, lights flip on and off and there have been a number of reports of guests seeing figures in medical attire hurrying about the third floor.

There have also been reports that a woman in white roams the halls and a nurse with a clipboard was seen in one man's room. There is a child who runs through the bar area looking for his mother late at night, and guests have reported hearing screaming and seeing apparitions on a regular basis.

Ghost City Inn

Figure 17: Ghost City Inn

Built around 1890 as a boarding house for lodging middle mine management, this building has seen many uses. In 1920, the Garcia family purchased the home and lived in it until 1959. Although most of its life has been spent as a boarding house, this Jerome building housed a still for a short time, served as an ashram and then as a restaurant called Maude's.

The building went through a major restoration project in 1994, and the current owners have renovated all the rooms in the last three years making a stay at the Ghost City Inn a unique experience. From the Victorian elegance of the Verde View Room to the rustic feel of a north woods cabin in the Northern Exposure Room the owners have made each room special and inviting. The building still carries some of the uneven floors and original beadboard ceilings.

A woman spirit, believed to be that of Grandmother Garcia has shown herself to visitors in the Cleopatra Room. This elderly lady, who during life lived in what is now the Cleopatra Room hated smoking. Those guests who like to smoke will often find their matches, lighters and cigarettes missing during their stay. Other guests have reported that they have felt that this spirit is actually protective and some have reported that they feel that she is tucking them in at night.

In the Northern Exposure Room, a guest reported feeling something invisible touching her face in the early hours of the morning. She then felt something try to pull the bed clothes off of her. There have also been reports of a male spirit wearing western garb seen in the hallways.

The Palace – Haunted Hamburger

Figure 18: The Palace - Haunted Hamburger

The Haunted Hamburger occupies a building on Clark Street that had sat empty for a number of years. Not a lot is known of its history other than it once been the Wykoff Apartments in the 1920s. No one is really sure of the identity of the ghost but he she or it does not seem to be evil, more mischievous. When the owner was renovating the building prior to opening, his hammer kept disappearing forcing him to purchase a new one each time. Then one day he comes to work and all three hammers were lying in a very prominent place. A repairman also reported that a wrench he was using while atop a ladder simply vanished, to appear in the kitchen. So for an excellent hamburger, and the chance to see a ghost, go to the Haunted Hamburger.

The Surgeon's House Bed and Breakfast

The building that houses the Surgeon's House Bed and Breakfast was built in 1916 for Jerome's Chief Surgeon, and has been on the National Historic Registry since 1966, and has a rich history. The property, on Hill Street in Jerome was originally the George W. Hull Homestead Tract. Mr. Hull was far-sighted and industrious, and obtained what became the town site of Jerome, Arizona and much of the surrounding mineral rights. When major companies wanted his interests, his price was one million dollars. The United Verde Copper Company paid it.

Figure 19: the Surgeon's House

On the site the Company built a new hospital and a virtual mansion for their Head Physician to live in. Arthur Kelly, noted Los Angeles architect, designed both with arched windows, gleaming stucco, and rich red tile roofs. All the modern comforts were included.

Used for years as the nurses' residence, in the early 1930's the house became home of the then Chief Surgeon, Dr. Arthur Carlson, and his family. Decorated with the finest, it became a warm and hospitable home. Parties were held to create a diversion for the Company's upper echelon from the hard work in this hard rock mining town.

After the closing of the mine in 1953, the house became home for the Company's agent, and later, other Jerome community members. Councilmen, mayors, merchants, geologists, policemen, even the local Jerome postmaster, all enjoyed the simple elegance of this house.

Though the house sat empty for many years, it was still inhabited by the ghosts of those who felt that this house was a suitable place to spend eternity. One of those is believed to be named Alice. Alice was actually the maid at the house that stood next door to the Surgeon's House, but she seems to have moved in and assumed those duties here. She has been seen numerous times, always wearing her blue uniform.

The owner, a lady, had reported that she has awoken to see a man wearing a suit and carrying a doctor's bag walk across the master suite and enter the bathroom. In a few minutes he will reappear, wearing pajamas, and cross the room where he gets into her bed. At this point he usually vanishes. Guests who have stayed in the master suite have reported seeing a couple dancing about the room before fading away.

The Inn at Jerome

Figure 20: Inn at Jerome

If you've ever wanted to stay in a haunted inn, then the Inn at Jerome might be just the place. Located at 309 Main Street, this charming eight guest room Inn has been lovingly restored to its original Victorian splendor.

Workers at the inn tell of a phantom cat that walks the halls and even leaves indentations on the beds where it sleeps! Maids recall objects being moved by unseen hands. The Lariat and Lace Room, which boasts a step up four poster bed and matching barnwood armoire once had the door of said armoire unexplainably flung off its hinges.

One of these "ladies of the evening" is said to haunt this building, located on Main Street. During the copper camp's heyday, it was said that more than 120 prostitutes plied their trade in Jerome. One of madams, Jennie Banters, was said to be the richest women in northern Arizona. The Inn at Jerome is Jennie's former home and while it is no longer a brothel, Jennie has remained behind. In fact, one of the eight rooms here is called the "Spooks, Ghosts and Goblins" room. Jennie and her phantom cat have frequently been reported in the house. The cat often vanishes before guests can pick her up and loves to brush against people in the kitchen. Jennie often moves things about in the kitchen as well and keeps the maid busy by rearranging furniture, moving objects and rotating the ceiling fan. Each of the eight rooms has its own name and style.

Radios turning on and off at will, laughter and voices can be heard coming from empty rooms and deserted hallway. Guests' personal items moved in the rooms. Rooms and Hallway have "cold spots" and at time extremely "hot spots". One lady guest came downstairs in the morning, stating that she had been in the bathroom with the door locked while she took her shower and loudly heard a man's laughter in the same bathroom. The building also has a ghost cat that will leave its pawprints and "curled up" impression on the bedspreads. It will rub on the legs of the guests in the restaurant and generally has a good time chasing mints from room to room. Impressions of human forms have also been seen on the beds.

In the Victorian Rose Room the vase which sits on the lace runner on the dresser flew through the air and crashed to the floor in the hallway. Guests have also reported the strong smell of perfume and even permanent solution flowing through the room.

Guest staying in the Heart Room had bolted the door before retiring and were sound asleep when the door silently opened to allow the light from the parlor to stream into the room. A moment later the door quietly closed. When they checked the door, it was found to be bolted. The action of locking the dead bolt is a noisy process.

In the Kiss And Tell Room the armoire doors fly open at will. Wall hangings and pictures are rearranged or placed in the armoire. During the Jerome Home Tours of 2000, the door between the parlor and hallway violently slammed closed 6 times. There is no possible way that it was caused by wind or air disturbance.

The Cherub statue on the dividing wall between the parlor and stairway is commonly observed turning with no one near it. This was one of the events that was noticed during a ghost hunting group's investigation. The statue is facing towards the door leading into the hallway. If it is turned facing the opposite direction, towards the stairs, it will mysteriously move back to its original position.

Jerome Inn and Grille Building

This section includes some more information about The Inn at Jerome as well as the Grille Building. The Inn at Jerome has eight guest rooms, designed in their original Victorian style popular around 1900. This Inn has a large parlor with a fireplace. The Inn's restaurant, The Jerome Grill, offers registered dietician approved American cuisine and heart healthy cuisine. The breakfasts that come with the guests' stay are highly rated and recommended.

This building, once known as the Clinksdale building, was built in 1899, made of poured, reinforced concrete. The walls were 18 inches thick, with the idea to make it as fire-proof as possible, as it was being built upon the ashes of a fire-destroyed building, the victim of the 3rd fire which hit Jerome.

It was once the home of Madam Jennie Banters' Bordello, a very popular place which earned a pretty penny in its day. When the ladies of the night were forced off the main street of town, the building was used as a hardware store on the bottom floor and the upper bedrooms on the second floor were turned into apartments. This building has been in continuous use ever since.

The upstairs rooms and hallway have cold and hot spots, locked doors are opened and closed, as well as other occurrences often attributed to entities abound in this very haunted building.

- Madam Jennie Banter was easily the wealthiest woman in town in her era, became active in the building after it was transformed into the Inn at Jerome, probably very pleased with the renovation efforts. Her favorite room seems to be the Lariat and Lace Room. She has rearranged the furniture, likes to play with the ceiling fan, and has been known to move items in the room to places of her choice, much to the annoyance of the maids, and to the surprise of the guests. She is kind to the maids by turning on the radio as they tidy up the room for the next guests.

- Jennie likes to keep an eye on the cook in the Grille kitchen, and lets her presence be known. She has made objects like ice cream scoops fly off their resting place onto the floor, if not put away properly? She made the cook books move by themselves until they fell on the floor. Perhaps she was trying to look up a recipe!

- There is a phantom cat from the past still claims the Inn at Jerome as home. It is thought to be Madam Jennie's pampered pet. Guests, employees and the managers of the Inn have felt the friendly kitty rub up against their legs. Its plaintive meows have been heard in various areas of the building. The sound of a cat sharpening its claws was heard, coming from a shelf, located above the doorway, as one enters the Inn at Jerome. This kitty is still taking naps on the beds in the guest rooms. The cat rolls up in a tight ball, making an indentation on the bed. This kitty appeared in the kitchen when he ran quickly from under the grill, once around the startled cook's feet and scampered away, vanishing into thin air.

- There is also an elderly male ghost that also haunts the building. It appears to be a friendly, gentle spirit, with a sense of humor, who has chosen the Inn at Jerome as his eternal retirement home. This spirit was seen by the manager as she walked down the hall past the guest rooms. She saw a hazy, grayish colored apparition of an elderly man, standing by the window in the room called Pillow Talk, looking down at the alley below. He was dressed in work clothes from an earlier time and wore a felt hat and has been known to laugh at the maids and the Inn managers, as well as some guests as well.

- After making the bed and straightening and smoothing the pillows and comforter in the rooms Pillow Talk and Kiss and Tell, the maid would leave for a moment and when she returned, she would find the indentation of a human body on the bed. She immediately redid the bed, only to find the same indentation when she checked the room again! The doors to the armoire in the Kiss and Tell Room seem to have a mind of their own, and open and close on their own schedule.

- There is also the spirit of a Grumpy Male Ghost. He is said to be an entity with some issues. Perhaps he isn't pleased with the renovations of the building, or that this Inn at Jerome and Grille Restaurant has moved into the building. There's always a critic! He gets his chuckles by startling the living, though he never hurts anyone. He likes to hang out in the upstairs area. Some of the things that has caused include a cold wind blew strongly through one of the guest rooms, removing the blankets off the startled guests. The windows were closed, and there was no reasonable explanation. While straightening up in the Victorian Rose Room, a maid saw a shadowy apparition of a man move across the room and go behind the door.

- The smell of roses, and sometimes of perfume, moves through the Victorian Rose Room, and the water faucets have been known to turn on and off in the sink at will.

- At the Jerome Grill a waitress on the early morning shift was alone in the restaurant, when she heard a man's footsteps walking up behind her. Thinking it was the cook, she turned around to talk to him. Instead, standing there was the shadowy apparition seen in the Victorian Room with a bad attitude, starring at her with cold, grumpy disapproval, with his head cocked to one side. After she screamed, it disappeared quickly. Whistling has also been heard in the bar area. In the kitchen, the cook was reaching down to pick up something off a lower shelf, when two plastic containers from a high shelf in the preparation area suddenly fell down and hit him in the head. While it didn't hurt him, it did shake him up a little.

- This grumpy ghost likes to eavesdrop on occasion on conversations in the Grille. When a skeptic verbally expressed to her group that the hauntings were a bunch of nonsense, a metal sign sitting up on a ledge above her suddenly flew down with a bang onto the floor.

There have also been other Jerome Grill Hauntings that could mean that there are other ghostly residents staying in the Inn at Jerome. Some of these include the following events:

- Glasses sitting on tables have been known to slide off by themselves with a crash. A waitress in the restaurant's rest room heard a woman singing, followed by a loud bang. No one else outside the bathroom heard this.

- Like entities everywhere, the ghost(s) that haunt the restaurant are fascinated with electric devices, especially the answering machine. After it was turned off after the restaurant had opened, the machine turned itself on three different times, much to the annoyance of the waitress in charge of turning it off when she arrived at work.

KINGMAN

Hotel Brunswick

Figure 21: Hotel Brunswick

The Hotel Brunswick was originally built in 1909. It was the first three story building for counties around. The Owners, Mulligan and Thompson earned the reputation of providing upscale services by using Waterford crystal stemware and solid brass beds. The Hotel Brunswick, even during its formative years provided guests with full electricity and telephones in every room.

Unfortunately, a rift between the partners (over a lady of course[6]) caused a division of the property in 1912. A wall was built to create two separate hotels. The separate hotels continued to operate, one side featuring a bar and 25 rooms and the other a restaurant and 25 rooms. In 1960, Joe

---

[6] The cause of the rift between the two partners eventually married Mulligan. She died of an illness and is now believed to be one of the ghosts that haunt the hotel.

Artero bought both hotels and tore down the wall separating the two establishments.

The first experience that the new owner, Gerard Gordon, had with the ghosts of the Hotel was in Room 312. Every time he walked into the room his hair would stand on end. The ghosts were also playing pranks on him. Finally, he put his foot down and told them to stop. Surprisingly, they did.

In Room 212 the spirit of an old gentleman has been seen. This is believed to be the spirit of 73 year old W.D. McCright who died in the room in 1915[7]. In 202 there is a ghost that likes to move things about which makes it tough on the housekeeping staff. Then there is the spirit of a little girl who wanders about the hotel leaving a trail of old pennies in her wake.

A German couple stayed in room 201 for a time. The woman came to tell him that a ghost had tried to pull her out of the bed by tugging on one of her legs. Her husband witnessed this bizarre occurrence.

The ghosts also seem determined to help Gerard manage the hotel. One night he was awoken by a sound that led him to a leaking pipe. He had the plumber in to repair this and to check for other problem with the plumbing.

---

[7] Kingman Daily Mirror, March 13, 1915.

Major renovation was called for, which would not have been done without his discovery of the leaking pipe.

NOGALES

Guevavi Mission

Guevavi is a name derived from the Pima word, gi-vavhia, meaning "big well" or "big spring." This settlement of Pima Indians was first visited in January 1691 by Jesuit Fathers Kino and Salvatierra. They established it as a mission, naming it San Gabriel de Guevavi. Subsequent missionaries called it San Rafael and San Miguel, resulting in the common historical name of Los Santos Angeles de Guevavi.

The Mission originally sat on land owned by the Wingfield family. The ranch headquarters is a sprawling collection of courtyards and interconnecting rooms that is located on a hill overlooking the corrals and two lakes. It is such a peaceful setting that one of Ralph Wingfield's close friends, John Wayne spent many a vacation in the cool of the Guevavi courtyards. In fact, the current owner believes that he has encountered the spirit of John Wayne, still enjoying the peace and quiet of the historic ranch.

Wayne liked to smoke unfiltered Lucky Strikes and on several occasions, the current owner has encountered the unmistakable odor of unfiltered cigarettes in the John Wayne Suite (See the picture on the next page) as well as in the corral. Perhaps, the Duke is just checking on the state of the old ranch, a place he once loved and enjoyed.

Ralph Wingfield walked away from this beautiful place when his spirit of broken by tragedy. In the space of one year, he lost a grandson to the waters of the lake on the property, his wife and his best friend, John Wayne to cancer. It was too much and this proud man walked away from a place that reminded him of such misery. Now it is a bed and breakfast.

Figure 22: The main house at Guevavi

In 1701, Guevavi was established as a district headquarters and Juan de San Martin was assigned as the first resident priest. A small church was started that same year. Father Martin left in 1703. Fathers Agustin de Campos and Luis Xavier Velarde visited occasionally after that. Father Grazhoffer, in 1732, reestablished Guevavi as cabecera and completed the church. Unfortunately, he died the following year - possibly of poison. Father Garrucho, resident priest from 1745 to 1751, recorded 148 burials, many from disease. In 1751, Father Garrucho contracted the building of a 15 foot by 50 foot church, the ruins of which still exist today.

    The first captain of the Tubac presidio, Juan Tómas de Beldarrain, was wounded by Seri Indians and died at Guevavi. His body lies buried beneath the altar steps of the church. The mother of Captain Juan Bautista de Anza, Beldarrain's replacement, is also buried in front of the altar.

Figure 23: The John Wayne Suite

The Pima revolt of 1751, later Apache raids, disease, and the removal of the Jesuits in 1767 caused much disruption to mission life. The first Franciscan, Juan Crisóstomo Gil de Bernabé, arrived in 1768 and began the mission with about fifty families. Unfortunately the Apaches attacked in 1769 and killed all but two of the few Spanish soldiers guarding the mission. In 1770 and 1771, the Apaches continued their attacks and the cabecera was moved to Tumacácori.

Father Antonio de los Reyes on 6 July 1772 submitted a report on the condition of the missions in the Upper and Lower Pimeria Alta. This was his report on Los Santos Angeles de Guevavi as translated by Father Kieran McCarty.

The village of Guevavi is situated on an open and fertile plain beside an arroyo with good land where the Indians cultivate their individual fields of wheat, Indian corn, other crops, ad one small community farm. The church on the inside is adorned with two altars and a small side chapel with paintings in gilded frames. In the sacristy are three chalices, two dishes with cruets, one pyx, a ciborium, a censer, and a baptismal shell - all silver - vestments of every kind and color and other ornaments for the altar and divine services. According to the census book, which I have here before me, there are nineteen married couples, five widowers, seven widows, twelve orphans, the number of should in all eighty-six.

Guevavi was abandoned for the last time in 1775. Now, after sitting forlornly abandoned since the 1770s, Guevavi's ruins were added to Tumacácori National Historical Park in 1990. Ralph Wingfield, a local rancher, donated the ruins to the New Mexico Archaeological Conservancy which, in turn, donated it to the National Park Service.

There are a number of stories about hidden treasure around the old mission and there have been a number of ghosts sighted near the old mission ruins. There has been the ghost of a conquistador at the main entrance who is probably the spirit of the first captain of the Tubac presidio, Juan Tómas de Beldarrain as well as several robed monks as well as a number of Indians. There is no doubt that the Old Mission at Guevavi is not abandoned, but is still populated by those who are doomed to spend eternity around its walls.

OATMAN

Oatman Hotel

Figure 24: The Oatman Hotel

The Oatman Hotel was originally built in 1902 as the Durlin Hotel. This historic old hotel has been destroyed once during a fire in 1924 and then rebuilt. This hotel is also where Clark Gable and Carole Lombard spent their wedding night[8] in Room 15. Over the years, the old hotel carried a number of names but was changed to the Oatman Hotel in the 1960s. When Route 66 was replaced with the interstate, Oatman again suffered a devastating blow and dwindled to just a few gift shops and restaurants. Today only about 100 people live in Oatman year-round.

The Oatman Hotel is one of the biggest attractions of the small village as the word of its mischievous ghosts has spread far and wide. The first and foremost ghosts are those of Clark Gable and Carole Lombard, who evidently had so many fine memories of the old hotel that they simply refuse to leave. Continuing to celebrate, guests and staff have often heard the pair whispering and laughing from the room when it is empty. According to one report, when a professional photographer took a picture of the empty room, the ghostly figure of a man appeared on the developed print.

Evidently Clark and Carole are not alone, as there are other spirits that reportedly haunt the old hotel. The second floor houses a Theater Room Museum where distinct outlines of sleeping bodies have been found in the dust on the beds. Upon closer inspection, none of the surrounding areas appear to be disturbed. Staff suspects

---

[8] March 29, 1939

that the sleeping spirit is that of a former chambermaid who has often been spotted in the room.

Another guest room is also said to be haunted by an Irish miner who once lived there. Distraught because his family died when on their way to America, he had a habit of heavy drinking. One night he got really carried away with the drinking passed out behind the hotel. He never woke up. It is said that he has haunted his old room in the hotel ever since. The staff refers to this spirit as "Oatie," who is often heard playing his bagpipe around the hotel. Other common pranks include opening the window in his former room and pulling the covers off of the bed. There have also been reports of the room being very cold in the midst of a hot desert day.

Downstairs in the saloon, it appears that there are several playful spirits at work here, who have been said to lift money off the bar and raise glasses into the air. Other strange phenomena include lights turning on and off seemingly by themselves, the sounds of eerie voices, toilets that flush in empty bathrooms and footprints that appear from nowhere on recently cleaned floors.

Lucky for the Oatman Hotel, it seems as if their bevy of unusual guests are the playful friendly type and don't make a habit of scaring away their guests.

ORACLE

Arcadia Ranch

The Acadia Ranch at Oracle was built by Edwin S. and Lillian Dodge around 1880 to raise sheep. Later it became a guest ranch and hotel. The first U.S. Post Office was established at the Acadia in 1880. Later, a bath house was added and the Acadia became a sanitarium for tuberculosis sufferers, who were referred to Oracle for its clean, fresh air and pleasant climate.

One of the ghosts is a nurse who contracted the disease and died. She is still trying to take care of people. There is another there that dislikes things hung on the north wall of the main room. There was artwork hung on the wall. In the evening went he caretaker left it would be on the wall, and in the morning it would be set on the floor.

PHOENIX

Arizona State Prison Complex - Flamenco Unit

Figure 25: Arizona State Prison

Arizona State Prison Complex– Phoenix is one of 13 prison facilities operated by the

Arizona Department of Corrections (ADC). ASPC-Phoenix is located in Phoenixn, Maricopa County, Arizona, which includes a minimum security unit near Globe, the Arizona Correctional Facility for Woman (ACW), and ASPC-Aspen[9].

The Phoenix Complex is a unique facility within the Department. Four of its units are on the grounds of the Arizona State Hospital and leased through the Department of Health Services. They are Alhambra Reception and Treatment Center, which opened in 1979, and handles all incoming male inmates. Reception has a design capacity of 207; another 40 beds are in B-Ward, the Treatment Center; and there are 30 beds designated for resident workers. The other units are Aspen DWI, a 200-bed facility which opened in 1983 for adult males incarcerated under the state Driving While Intoxicated (DWI) law; Flamenco Mental Health Center, a licensed 105-bed psychiatric hospital for adult males which opened in 1985; and Flamenco Health Center for Women, a licensed 20-bed behavioral hospital for adult females which opened in 1990.

Two other units are separated geographically but considered part of the Phoenix Complex. One, the Arizona Center for Women at 32nd Street and East Van Buren, has a designated capacity of 250; it opened in 1979, originally

---

[9] From Wikipedia, the free encyclopedia.

under a lease arrangement, and is now owned by the Department. The other is ASP-Globe, a 150-bed prison for adult males which was originally Pinal Mountain Juvenile Institution; it was legislatively transferred to ADC on July 1, 1991.

The Flamenco Unit was built in 1920 and was for years a division of the state hospital. It is now used to house inmates with mental health issues. Numerous patients and inmates have died in the facility over the years, and now at night you can hear keys rattle, (most officers think another officer has entered the area only to find that no one is there and everyone is accounted for on other units) an unknown woman is seen in the female units library, doors open and close on their own, and very often extra inmates are counted, and when rechecked they are not there. It is not unusual to undercount the number and need to recount, but with inmates locked in their rooms, it is very difficult to count one twice. You can miss someone who is in a non visible corner, but extra inmates just don't happen.

Billington House

The youngest daughter has reported almost all the sightings at the Billington House. She has heard footsteps and people talking while she has been home alone. She has seen a glowing figure of a person with one arm standing in the second-floor window of her playhouse. She said that it stood motionless, and that she only saw it at night. She saw it three nights in a row. She told her dad one night, and he looked out the window by her bed to the tree house directly where she said it was standing and did not see a thing. On the fourth night there was no such person in the tree house, as if it had never been there at all. The same child has awoken in the night and looked out her window to see a man in a long black coat and a hat standing on her patio. She closed her eyes for no more than a second and when she opened them the man was gone. She has also seen a woman looking at her and smiling at her from her closet.

San Carlos Hotel

Figure 26: San Carlos Hotel

The land upon which the San Carlos Hotel is built has long been important to the city of Phoenix. On this spot Native Americans once worshipped their god of wisdom. It was also upon this spot where the first school house in Phoenix was constructed in 1874. In 1879 that original one room school building was replaced by a two story brick building with a bell tower.

At the same time that the original school house was built, a well was dug that happened to correspond with the center of an energy vortex held sacred by the Indians. That well still exists in the basement of the San Carlos Hotel which was built in 1928.

Along with all of the history that surrounds this historic old hotel, there are also several ghosts who seem content to spend eternity wandering the halls of this elegant hotel.

The most famous, of course, is the ghost of a young lady who is believed to have committed suicide. Her name was Leone Jenson, 22, who is believed to have jumped from the roof of the seventh floor at 2:45 A.M. on May 7, 1928[10]. Her body was found on the Monroe Street side of the hotel and it was believed that death was instantaneous. Her remains were taken to Merryman's Mortuary.

Though a scream had been heard by a guest in the hotel as Miss Jensen leaped to her death, the way in which she fell was very extraordinary. She did not land in a heap;

---

[10] This story is from the Arizona Republic, May 7, 1928.

rather her body was in a very neat position as if she had lain down on the sidewalk to sleep. She was wearing a very smart evening gown of the very best material. Her shoes were also some of the best available at the time. It would appear that she had money, though only five cents was found on her body.

At the time of her death, Miss Jensen had been at the San Carlos for only two days, having come there from another hotel in town. Two death notes were found in the room inn which she was registered, Room 720. In one of these she mentioned a bell boy at another hotel. It was believed that she had a romance with this young man, but she caught him in the arms of another woman. The second note asked that Mr. Jack Edwards an undertaker in Los Angeles be notified of her death so that he could make the arrangements for her body. Other than being rejected by the Bell Boy she was said to have a romance with, there was no reason for her suicide found, though there were rumors that she was pregnant by the Bell Boy.

Since that time the window of Room 720 cannot be opened, through there have been many reports of a flowery scent being detected throughout the room as well as the hallway. Many guests have also reported seeing her gown float in the room and many have smelled the perfume that she wore. Some have even heard her cry and moan in the early hours of the morning.

Leone Jensen is not the only ghost to make the San Carlos their home. Many guests have heard the running footsteps and laughter of young boys who are believed to have attended Central Elementary School which stood on the spot now occupied by the San Carlos.

Tapatio Cliffs Resort- The Point Hilton

Figure 27: The Point Hilton

The Pointe Hilton Tapatio Cliffs Resort sits astride the dramatic peaks of [11]the Phoenix North Mountains and just 20 minutes from the Sky Harbor Airport. There are reports that the main ballroom is haunted by a drunken man who, when at a wedding reception some 20 years ago reportedly walked up to the cliffs right behind the ballroom, and fell head first off the edge of the cliff to his death. As told by a couple of security guards there, the spirit of this unhappy man haunts the boiler room, and no one is allowed down there after midnight.

PRESCOTT

Hassayampa Inn

Figure 28: Hassayampa Inn

The Hassayampa Inn was built in 1927 in Prescott. Prescott had been the territorial capital since 1864 and the demand for hotel rooms was high. A honeymoon couple checked into the hotel shortly after it opened. The newlyweds were placed in Room 426 and seemed a happy couple. However, one evening the husband went out for cigarettes and never returned. The new bride, who name is known only as Faith, kept a vigil for her husband for several days before committing suicide by hanging. Among her belongings were her clothes and an unpaid bill. Apparently he left her with no money. Now she haunts the scene of her demise making Room 426 the most haunted room in the hotel.

However, Room 426 is not the only haunted room in the hotel. A former manager has had a number of encounters with a female spirit when she lived in Room 2. The spirit would disturb her almost every night so that she finally moved into another room. The disturbances stopped.

One of the maids encountered something unusual every time she would go to clear Room 27. She reported that it was a male presence that would follow her around the room as she cleaned. His attention made her feel very uncomfortable.

There was also a presence in Room 19 who would spend a great deal of time each day sweeping the hardwood floor in the room. The sound of the broom on the floor was so loud that it could be heard in the office directly below.

In Room 402, two guests reported that they secured the door with the do not disturb sign on the outside doorknob. In spite of the three locks, they woke up during the night twice to find the door open and the do not disturb sign on the inside knob.

A guest in 426 reported that he had felt a presence in the room that seemed to be watching him. Finally, he fell asleep to awaken to the sensation of arms around him. When he sat up the sensation ceased, but his girlfriend, asleep on the other side of the bed had not been the one to put her arms around him. A maintenance worker in the hallway saw Faith come down the hall wearing a pink gown and disappear into the room. However, when he followed her into the room it was empty.

There are also stories of a small girl spirit haunting the kitchen. She will cut the gas burners off and on at odd times and generally cause chaos.

One evening the front desk received a call from Room 449. However, during the renovation Room 449 was merged into another room and no longer existed.

There is also the story of the Night Watchman, a spirit who will materialize in the bar area and make a complete circuit of all of the downstairs doors to jiggle the knob to make sure that they are locked. Once he has made his round and knows that all is secure, he will fade away.

Hotel Vendome

Figure 29: Hotel Vendome

The best known spirit to inhabit the historic Hotel Vendome is Abigail Byr, who is said to have died in Room 16 in 1921. There are several version of the story about Abigail. In one, she was the owner who lost the hotel due to taxes in another she was the manager. However, most seem to believe that she and her husband were tenants.

Abigail was said to have been ill with tuberculosis and spent most of her time in bed in Room 16 with her cat, Noble. Her husband spent his time caring for his ailing wife. One night, her condition worsened and her husband went out to get medicine and never returned. Abigail locked herself in her room and refused to either come out or even eat. Shortly both she and Noble died of starvation, though it was some time before the bodies were discovered. Noble was buried in the back yard of the hotel and Abby went to potters field.

The ghost of Abigail Byr began to appear after World War II. Since her first appearance there has been a great deal of activity. The television, the ceiling fans and the lights will flip on and off. The faucets in the bathroom turn on and off and there are small puddles of water that mysteriously appear about the room.

Other guests have heard what sounds like a cat scratching on the inside of the closet door trying to get out. However, when they look, there is nothing in the closet. Others have heard a cat meowing or purring loudly from the area around the bed. A stuffed white cat that is part of the room's furnishings was moved from the bed to a chair by the guest. The next morning, the stuffed cat was found curled up on the floor as if asleep. There have also been reports of personal items that were inside suitcases being found scattered about the room.

The hauntings are not confined to just Room 16. Guests in Room 10 witnessed a figure walk through their door in the early hours of the morning. Noble the cat has been known to go from Room 16 to Room 17. On one occasion when this is thought to have happened, the guest in Room 17, who had an allergy to cat hair, suffered an allergy attack.

Abby and her cat Noble began to make their presences known around World War II and have continued to this day. They basically haunt room 16, though she has been known to venture out to check up on the living. The current owners have a large binder which holds information, sightings, manifestations of Abby and Noble. Below are just a sample listed in the notebook.

Sample of Occurrences which have happened inside room 16:

- The closet hangers have been heard moving by themselves, and the sound of a cat toy being played with can be heard as well.
- Guests have experienced objects being moved when they are not looking, being touched softly by unseen presences, hearing or feeling Noble or Abby sitting on the bed, the smell of a strong perfume and feeling a gentle cool breeze blow past them in the room.
- Abby will occasionally make a visual appearance and has spoken to guests when they're in a sleep state.

- Spirit orbs have been photographed in the dark in room 16 by psychic researchers Dr. Oesten and Dr. Gill.

Occurrences which happened outside room 16.

- Footsteps have been heard in room 16, which traveled down the hall, and descended down the stairs to the lobby.
- Maids, while cleaning up the various rooms, sometimes have the TV on while they work. They have reported that Abby will turn down the sound on the TV, if she doesn't like the program being watched, listened to but will turn the sound back up if the living will switch channels. She hates MTV!

- Above the entrance to the Vendome, spirit entities have been seen in various forms.

Lynx Creek Farm Bed & Breakfast - Sharlot Hall

The Lynx Creek Farm Bed & Breakfast is located in a somewhat secluded location just a short drive from Prescott. The Montana lodge pole log cabin has two beautifully decorated guest rooms with king size beds and private baths with tubs and showers. The Guest House has two guest rooms that have woodstoves and private baths; both of the rooms open onto a large deck and hot tub. The

Lower Cabin guest rooms have king size beds, in room coffee, and private baths.

Guests have reported feeling cold spots, and have experienced the feeling of not being alone. Most agree that there is a definite presence in this room. The portrait in this room does not help since the eyes seem to follow you wherever you go in the room.

TOMBSTONE

Buford House

When the author first went to Tombstone over ten years ago, it was not as sophisticated as today. There are now several hotels as well as a number of bed and breakfast establishments. One of these is the Buford House Bed and Breakfast. This Bed and Breakfast is an 1880 adobe home that is listed on the National Register of Historic Places. The house was named after George Buford who was a prominent mine owner in that time. This house has been home to two sheriffs, a mayor, a state senator and various other people of local fame as well as the Duke, the famous John Wayne.

Figure 30: Picture given to the author in Tombstone.

Like much of Tombstone, this adobe home seems to be haunted by restless spirits. There is a strange light that has been reported being seen outside the upstairs bedroom from within, but there is no outside source for it. A guest staying in that same room saw an apparition of an old lady in the room who looked real enough that the guest informed her she was in the wrong room and would have to go. The spirit told the guest this was her room and that he had to leave. There is no record as to how this standoff ended, but it is rare that the ghost loses. I guess it comes down to first come first served and the ghost has been in the room longer. Lavender scent has also been smelled in the house. Perhaps it was the old woman's?

The story of the old woman did not surprise the owners, the Allens, as it was reported that the previous owners had reported seeing this spirit. They have another playful ghost that likes to play hide and seek with items. They tell of one instance where a woman was visiting with her family and her wallet was suddenly missing from her purse. The unfortunate guest and her family searched and searched but could never find the missing wallet. Finally, they decided to try again before leaving and to their surprise, found it under the bed with money, cards, everything...intact. They were all sure that the wallet wasn't under the bed when they searched earlier, before but it was there now!

The Allens, who run the Inn, have also witnessed another ghost who haunts their home. The spirit of George Davis is reported to have appeared one holiday season to admire their Christmas tree as they were setting it up. According to the legend, George Davis had lived in the house long ago and was in love with the girl by the name of Pietra[12], who lived across the street. He seems to be fairly active around the house, pulling small pranks such as turning lights on and off, and ringing the doorbell at 3am

---

[12] Petra's real name was Cleopatra Edmunds.

(no one is ever there when the Allens go look), and rapping on walls or windows[13].

According to the story of George Davis, at about 2 PM on that particular day[14], passersby on Third Street near Safford, saw George Davis chasing Cleopatra "Pietra" Edmunds, the 17 year old daughter of Eugene Edmunds and a Mexican mother. What attracted their attention was not the fact that he was chasing her, but the fact that he was firing at her with his six shooter. He apparently was not a very good shot for he only managed to hit her in the shoulder with one of his shots. At this point, apparently thinking that he had killed her, he then placed his gun to his own temple and fired one shot into his own brain. He died within minutes. Amazingly enough, Pietra survived her wound, making a full recovery.

A later investigation revealed that the cause of this altercation had been jealousy. George Davis had been courting Miss Edmunds for some months. The two were not formally engaged, but George believed that they had an "understanding". However, he was a miner and had been gone to his claim at Casa Grande for some weeks. Upon his return, he found that someone else had been courting Miss

---

[13] Tombstone Epitaph, "*A Bloody Tragedy*", April 14, 1888.
[14] Friday, April 13, 1888.

Edmunds in his place. This had resulted in a quarrel between the two.

On the day of the shooting, Miss Edmunds had been in the company of Mr. Fred Stone, the man that had been courting her in the absence of Mr. Davis. The two of them had occasion to pass in front of Mr. Davis' father's house where Mr. Davis was then visiting. Davis spotted them and came running out of the house waving his pistol. Miss Edmunds had screamed and began to run toward her own home while Stone, rather than try to defend Miss Edmunds, had taken off running toward the center of town and the Sheriff's office. Davis ran after Miss Edmunds and fired the shot that struck her in the back.

Like others who died tragic deaths, George continues to walk the earth, apparently lost in space and time. Both the owners and guests at the Buford House have seen him walking inside the home, as well as along the street in front of the old adobe structure. If anyone approaches him, he fades away or walks quickly out of sight.

Other phenomenon involves the doorbell ringing in the middle of the night, seemingly, of its own accord. Others have reported hearing knocking on walls, faucets turning themselves on and off, and strange lights appearing inside the rooms. Once in a while, women report that that they have felt someone touch their hair or stroke the back of their necks when no one else is around.

There are no records to indicate that Wyatt Earp or any of his brothers or the Clantons or McLaury's stayed here. This house was too respectable for them as they frequented staying on the main strip of town with its honky-tonks and bars[15]. The upstairs bedrooms are filled with antiques. Each room has a theme. The Wicker, Victorian and Western bedrooms share two bathrooms but have sinks in each room. The "Nellie Cashman" (named for a woman who readily gave food, shelter or money to people who were down on their luck) has a private bath. Downstairs is the Garden Room which has a gas log fireplace, private entrance and private bathroom with an original sunken, tiled, concrete bathtub.

This house has wonderful charm that you notice once you enter its doorway. There is a wood stairway that leads you up to the upper floor rooms and wooden armoires holding antiques as you enter. According to all reports, the owners, Ruth and Richard Allen, are the most accommodating people you can find. They are gracious and

---

[15] The Buford House Bed and Breakfast is at 2nd and Safford Streets in Tombstone, phone: (520) 457-3969.

hospitable and make you feel as though their home is your home. Although Mrs. Allen feels there are no malevolent or evil spirits in the house, she feels she needs to protect it. Thus, she has placed rosary beads at the bottom of the stairs.

Victorian Garden's Bed and Breakfast

Located next door to the Tombstone Courthouse Museum, the Victorian Garden's Bed and Breakfast is certainly worth visiting. Unfortunately on the two occasions that this author stopped by, there was no one about.

Figure 31: The front of Victorian Garden's Bed and Breakfast.

In the 1880's Emily Morton originally owned the building, and reportedly ran a 'house of pleasure' from within the walls. Back then the house originally consisted of four rooms, which appear to be the center of the haunting events which occur here. People report the sounds of shuffling papers, akin to someone working with a paper bag. The chandeliers have been known to swing about, and in one startling incident, the dining room table began to move, sliding along the floor and pinning one frightened woman against a piano. Black shadowy figures are sighted lurking throughout the home, and previous owners of the building have reported being woken at 3am to the smell of coffee and breakfast being cooked.

"Tombstone is full of spirits but it has some unhappy campers," said Victoria Collins, who owned Victoria's Bed & Breakfast and Wedding Chapel at the time of the interview. "They think the O.K. Corral should die already. They would like to just rest in peace and they're upset that there's always tourists around."

At her Tombstone business, "spirit activity of the ornery sort surfaces from time to time, and tales of ghosts in bygone days are documented." Collins said. However, among the uncanny occurrences at her Bed & Breakfast- chandeliers have swung, things have fallen off shelves, shadows have passed between people, and there have sightings of cat's eyes and black skulls on the wall -- none have been malicious. Collins isn't afraid of ghost tales hurting her business. The proprietor keeps books detailing every account of spiritual presence in the Bed & Breakfast in every room.

Tombstone Boarding House

The Tombstone Boarding House consists of two 1880 adobe houses surrounded by an 1880 style picket fence. The first house is known as the Blackburn house. In a 19th Century Photo, the south wall of the building was

Figure 32: The Tombstone Board House

covered by the Tombstone Rose. The home was remodeled and enlarged in the early 1930's. In 2000 the home was refurbished to create the Lamplight Room Restaurant, Tombstone's 1st Fine Dining experience in the New Millennium.

The second house was the original Barrows house where, according to legend, in the 1880's the notorious Buckskin Frank Leslie roomed. While proving to his wife that he could shoot drunk or sober, he shot her silhouette in the wall which was later plastered over.

In the 1930's, renowned artist H.E. Wenk built a studio addition with a large picture window framing a spectacular view of the surrounding mountains and Sheep's Head. There are a number of stories about the building originally known as the Barrows Boarding House. This adobe building was built in 1880 by Tombstone's first bank manager and then remodeled and enlarged in the early 1930s. At the time I was told this story it was the home to Shirley and Ted Villarin, owners of the Tombstone Boarding House[16].

According to legend, Billy Clanton, one of the three that died in the gun fight at the O.K. Corral which occurred on October 16, 1881, may well be responsible for this haunting. Even though it is said by many that Billy Clanton died at the scene of the gunfight, one account states that Billy didn't die of his injuries right away, but was taken to a nearby building for treatment. Some believe that it was the White Room in the Barrows Boarding House where he screamed in agony until he was given morphine for his pain. Although the medicine calmed him down, his heart

---

[16] The people that told me this story attributed it to Ellen Robson, Haunted Arizona: The Ghosts of the Grand Canyon State.

gave way before any other treatment could be administered and he died.

According to Shirley Villarin, there are two incidents that have occurred in the White Room to her knowledge. She reported that a young couple had checked in for two separate stays always asking for the White Room in the hopes of an encounter with Billy. On their third visit they happily reported over breakfast that they saw him. Shirley's said that her secretary just couldn't resist. She dashed off to the White Room and returned very excited with the news that she had seen him very clearly in the bathroom."

On another occasion, a close friend of Shirley's spent the night and spotted a young blond-haired man in the White Room. She also felt the presence of a young woman who was begging the gentleman not to go to the window or door. She sensed that there was an angry crowd outside, ready to lynch him.

The Green Room is the perfect place for anyone who welcomes dreams. Two women spent the night there once-several weeks apart - and experienced the same, vivid dream. The two guests independently reported that a young woman dressed in Victorian attire and a man wearing a duster and Western hat walked through their room. The dream ended with the couple continuing through the door and into a garden that was covered by a trellis with climbing roses.

During the filming of a movie, Ghosts of Tombstone, producers stayed in the Gold Room and got some special effects that weren't in the script. In the middle of the night, they were awakened to the sound of someone walking. But much to their dismay, there wasn't anyone around who could be held accountable for the mysterious footsteps.

Two ghosts have also been spotted by a guest in the main house-the apparition of a mother and what looked like her daughter, polishing furniture in the family room.

There are several rooms to choose from if you want to try to mingle with the spirits at the Tombstone Boarding House. But if you'd like some help with your housework, try to convince Shirley to allow you to throw down a sleeping bag in her family room in hopes that mother and daughter will follow you home!

Best Western Lookout Lodge

The Best Western Lookout Lodge is a place to be enjoyed. On the edge of one of the most famous old west towns in history, it also has excellent views of the Dragoon Mountains and most importantly, a resident ghost or ghosts. According to a number of stories, the owner has asked several ghost hunting groups to look into the happenings at the motel. According to the story, the manager has been told by some of the

Figure 34: The offices of the Lookout Lodge

housekeeping staff that there are ghosts in rooms 108 and

Figure 33: This is the magnificent view from the front of the Outlook Lodge.

208. These rooms are situated one above the other. The maids have reported seeing the lights in the upper room, #208, go on or off and on occasion, the TV would turn on or off when they went inside to clean the room. According to the maids if they told the ghost to stop doing those things in 208, it would actually stop, but then it would begin in 108.

It was also reported to me that some of the maids had reported seeing what looked like half a man, just the upper torso, appear in front of them in 208. Most of these stories seem to originate with the older staff members, though the current staff is certainly aware of the stories. Are rooms 208 and 108 haunted? You will only find out that answer if you are fortunate enough to stay in them. According to one maid that spoke to me for just a moment, the strange happenings are still taking place, only not as often.

Maricopa Resident Hall
University of Arizona

There are many tales of ghosts and unexplainable

Figure 35: Maricopa Resident Hall, University of Arizona

phenomena circulating the University of Arizona[17]. With a campus that's cluttered with old, brick buildings and plumbed with state-of-the-ancient toilets and faucets, that might not be surprising. Within the UA community, encounters with the supernatural have become as unpredictable as running into a creepy pervert.

One the UA's most infamous stories is about the ghost of Maricopa Residence Hall. Urban legend has it that a resident killed herself there. The circumstances

---

[17] From Myth or Reality? Ghosts at the UA by Nathan Tafoya, Arizona Daily Wildcat, Friday, October 31, 2003.

surrounding her death, however, change depending on the person talking about it.

Susan Metzger, an art history senior and former Maricopa resident, said the story she heard was based on the premise of the hall being the UA president's mansion.

"The version I heard was that his daughter was engaged to be married and she found her fiancé with another woman, and so she hung herself," Metzger said. "I've heard it was on the third floor and I've heard it was on the second floor and I've heard it was in the basement. So it's random."

The hall was first proposed by UA President Arthur Herbert Wilde in 1914 and constructed between 1918 and 1921; however, it was never the president's mansion.

"I've never seen the ghost when I lived here," Metzger said. "My friend Danielle said she saw her, but I think she was drunk."

Maricopa's basement is no tipsy joke though. "The basement here is really, really scary," Metzger said. "It has a bunch of locked doors. Nothing leads to anything, just storage stuff."

Associate Director of Residence Life Patrick Call has occupied the hall in past summers and said there are people who swear they have seen the ghost. "I never saw her," he said. "I would have liked to, but I never did."

Old Main's custodian, Andy Martinez, has heard more than just rumors during his late night shifts cleaning the UA's oldest building. Martinez said he has seen clocks fall off of the wall and heard water fountains recharge when he was the only person in the creaky building. But one thing in particular has given him the chills every night for the past month and a half.

Martinez said around 10 p.m. one night, he was standing next to a wall on the second floor, when he heard a knock. Martinez said he stood still for a moment and looked at the glass door leading outside, knowing all the doors behind him were locked. He did not see anyone. Then he heard a second knock.

"I knew nobody was at the door and I knew nobody was here," he said. "And of course there's nobody back there. I mean, it's just storage." Martinez pointed behind the wall located in the heart of the building. Martinez said he stood still in the hallway again, looking at the wall until he heard a third knock.

"And I was like, "Wait a minute, I know I'm not hearing things,'" he said. Martinez then yelled at the unknown knocker to come in, and the knocking stopped.

Since that night, Martinez said he gets freaked out when he passes by the area.

Some ghosts give a more theatrical performance when they decide to spook members of the UA community.

"There are reportedly ghosts throughout the Marroney Theatre that I've had a few encounters with and that students have had encounters with as well," said theatre arts associate professor Jeff Warburton.

Warburton said students have seen "Gene the Ghost" during theatrical performances.

Gene Lafferty was Warburton's predecessor, whom Warburton replaced as technical director. Warburton said he has heard steps in the theatre when he was there by himself and has experienced cold gusts of air brush over him.

One time, he lost his keys and was alone in the auditorium when he heard his keys fall from an audience seat. From jinxed productions like "The Crucible," to bad omens and phrases like "break a leg," the stage has always been a little superstitious.

"I think artists are more sensitive than people," Warburton said, explaining why this might be. But he does not believe ghosts hurt anyone. "They're not harmful at all," he said. "You usually hurt yourself running like hell."

Other scary campus stories have a lighter tone to them. Some students in the stadium residence halls have designated room 480 to "Harry the Ghost."

According to Michelle Ruppelt, a nutritional sciences junior, room 480 is an unfinished facility not large enough to be a dorm room and too small to be anything else.

"It was kind of a joke," Ruppelt said. "There's supposedly an unidentified ghost running around."

Ruppelt said the stadium residence halls have empty elevator shafts and unexplainable drafts and noises, which add to an overall feeling of eeriness. She said has not seen anything supernatural though.

TUCSON

Hotel Congress

The Hotel Congress was built in 1919 to serve the needs of the growing cattle industry as well as the many passengers of the Southern Pacific. The Hotel Congress of the 1920s was the perfect shelter for genteel travelers and high-rollers fresh from the east. It might have continued as just another place of lodging for road weary guests, if not for the date of January 22, 1934 has forever stamped its historical mark upon this edifice.

Figure 36: Hotel Congress

A fire started on the basement of the hotel and spread up the elevator shaft on the third floor. This fire led to the capture of one the country's most notorious criminals John Dillinger. After a series of bank robberies, the Dillinger Gang had come to Tucson to lay low. The gang resided on the third floor under aliases. After the desk clerk contacted them through the switchboard[18] the gang members escaped by aerial ladders.

On the urgent request of the gang, and encouraged by a generous tip, two firemen retrieved their heavy luggage. It was later discovered that the bags contained a small arsenal of weapons as well as $23,816 in cash. Later these same two firemen recognized the gang in a true detective magazine. A stakeout ensued and the gang members were captured at a house on North Second Ave in the space of five hours, without firing a single shot. To the embarrassment of the federal authorities, the police of small town Tucson had done what the combined forces of several states and the FBI had tried so long to do. When captured, Dillinger simply muttered, "Well, I'll be damned".

However, along with being associated with the capture of John Dillinger, the Hotel Congress is also associated with several ghosts. One of the rooms in the hotel is haunted by a man who had a heart attack and died. He has been seen looking out of the window.

Room 242 is known as the Suicide Room, a name given to it a few years ago, when a troubled woman shot herself in the bathroom after a standoff with the police and

---

[18] The original switchboard is still in operation at the hotel.

a SWAT team. People staying in this room often hear strange noises that are quite creepy and they often have nightmares involving bloody suicides. The ghost of this woman has also been seen in the bathroom and in the hallway outside of her room.

Pioneer International Hotel

Figure 37: Pioneer International Hotel

The Pioneer International Hotel is located at the corner of Stone and Pennington Streets. Tucson received national attention in 1970 for fire at the Pioneer International Hotel, in which 29 people died. The tragedy began to unfold around midnight on Dec. 20, 1970[19].

The landmark Downtown hotel was packed with guests visiting to shop or celebrate the holidays. Included in

---

[19] Volante, Eric, <u>New Scientific Knowledge of How Fire Behaves is Raising Questions About Whether Tucson's 1970 Pioneer International Hotel Fire Stemmed from Arson; New Probe Is Sought for Hotel Fire that Killed 29</u>. The Arizona Daily Star, TucsonMcClatchy-Tribune Business News

those present were many prominent citizens from Arizona and Sonora, Mexico.

At a party on the ground floor, bandleader Louis Leon and other musicians caught the faint smell of burning. They thought the wires to their sound equipment must be overheating. Then the catering manager approached with a terse message that he wanted the bandleader to "get them the hell out of here. The place is on fire."

Leon recalled recently that guests filed out in an orderly manner. The bandleader went outside to move his car and looked up. "You could see the flames coming out of the hotel windows," he said. "Boy, that was really a nightmare."

Old photos, interviews with witnesses and newspaper accounts paint a black picture of that night. A few guests clambered down a fire-escape tower. But acrid smoke and withering heat -- fueled mainly by the synthetic carpet that covered the floors and lower walls of the hallways -- spread rapidly through the top eight floors of the 11-story building and trapped others. As firefighters raced to the hotel, they listened to radio reports of people leaping from windows near Alameda Street.

One woman clung to a pipe outside her window. Some guests threw mattresses out windows, then jumped, only to be crushed against the pavement. Up in Room 722, a mother and her five children perished.

On the ninth floor, a gray-haired woman leaned out of a window at the rear of the hotel. She yelled again and again to firefighters, "I'm still here! My God, I'm still here! Minutes later, she plunged to her death.

On the 10th floor, a 31-year-old attorney, Paul E. d'Hedouville, died from carbon-monoxide fumes in his windowless room.

Businessman Harold Steinfeld, who had owned the hotel since 1929, and his wife, Peggy, were in their penthouse suite on the 11th floor.

"My husband talked to them (by phone) that night," the Steinfelds' niece, Bettina Lyons, recalled last week. "They said everything was fine, not to worry, the fire would be put out. They had heard from the desk downstairs that if they needed to, they'd come and get them."

After rescuers battled their way to the penthouse, one announced by radio that they thought that they had found Mr. and Mrs. Steinfeld. When asked if they were OK, the response was negative.

The couple, overcome by smoke, and 26 other people died. Another woman died months later of her injuries, bringing the toll to 29.

The tragedy tore the hearts of families on both sides of the U.S.-Mexican border.

The hotel "never recovered again. Even though they put money into it and put sprinkler systems in, people did not come to stay," Lyons said.

"And because the Pioneer Hotel was lost, all the people who came to shop Downtown did not come there. And one by one the stores began to die. So I would say it had an enormous effect on Downtown and the community. It probably changed it irreparably. And it's still struggling."

Rebuilt after a fire killed trapped occupants on the upper floors, it is said that the hotel is haunted by the spirits of those who died in the fire. Witnesses have reported hearing strange sounds, smelling smoke and seeing people trying to escape the flames.

Radisson Hotel

The Radisson Hotel on East Speedway in believed to be haunted by a woman that was murdered by her boyfriend when he found out she was seeing another man in the hotel. Witnesses have reported seeing and hearing a ghost of a girl in the kitchen and around the ballroom area. She seems to be crying or moaning for help.

WILLIAMS

Red Garter Bed and Bakery

Figure 38: Red Garter Bed and Bakery

The building that houses the Red Garter Bed and Bakery was built in 1897 by August Tetzlaff, a German tailor, Tetzlaff planned to cash in on the expected silver and copper boom anticipated at the Grand Canyon. The building first a housed a saloon on the first floor and a brothel with a parlor and eight cribs upstairs, where the girls were often known to hang out of the windows calling to the working men below. A steep flight of stairs known as the "Cowboy's Endurance Test" led to the girls upstairs rooms. The second floor also boasted a two-story outhouse off the back of the building, so that brothel "guests" wouldn't have to navigate the steep stairs once again.

Behind the saloon, two rear rooms of the building once housed Chinese railroad workers, who both lived and operated a chophouse and opium den crowded into the small space. During this time, the local sheriff was often called to the site to investigate a murder, only to arrive to find nothing out of the ordinary. At one point, the tales became so frequent, that the local garbage collector was lowered into the cesspool below the outhouses to look for bodies, only to be lifted again, having found nothing[20].

The saloon was operated for years by a man named Longino Mora, who was a notable figure as a U.S. Cavalry Scout and well known for his heroism in the Indian Wars. Born in 1848 in Socorro, New Mexico, Longino also became legendary in Williams for having five wives and twenty-five children over the years. When his youngest child was born, his oldest child was sixty years old. The saloon and bordello thrived as miners, loggers, cowboys, and railroad workers stopped in for a drink and often to partake of the painted ladies upstairs.

By the turn of the century, Williams had gained a reputation as a rough and rowdy frontier town, filled with saloons, brothels, gambling houses, and opium dens. Soon,

---

[20] The Red Garter Bed & Bakery in Williams, Arizona is reportedly haunted by the ghost of Eva. April, 2005, Kathy Weiser

the town restricted the houses of vice to an area called "Saloon Row" on Railroad Avenue.

Though Arizona outlawed prostitution in 1907, the law was only loosely enforced. Even during prohibition, the saloon and brothel continued to operate, hiding its bar and poker tables behind a divider. Both businesses continued to operate successfully until the mid 1940s, when a murder was committed on the stairs of the Red Garter, leading to a city-wide crackdown on houses of ill-repute. The crackdown ultimately led to the closure of the saloon and brothel after more than forty years of operation.

Over the next several decades the building would house different types of businesses, including a rooming house and general store. In 1979, a man by the name of John Holst bought the building but continued to lease it out until 1994. At that time, Holst renovated the building converting the eight cribs into four guest rooms, each with its own bathroom, and opened the Red Garter Bed and Bakery.

After opening, guests and staff began to report signs of ghostly activity, including the sound of footsteps when no one is around, doors mysteriously slamming, and strange "clunking" noises heard throughout the building. Though one might think that the spiritual activity could be attributed to the murder that occurred on the stairway or the many missing people during the Chinese opium days, the spirit is said to actually be that of a young girl, for which no one can account for.

Guests have reported seeing the apparition, describing her as a Hispanic girl with long dark hair and dressed in a white nightgown. One guest who claimed to have made contact with the spirit, said her name was Eve or Eva.

While most guests of the historic inn report getting a good night's sleep, others have said they felt their beds shake or someone touching their arms.

The most unusual phenomena is that the ghost seems to sometimes appear in photographs. One such photograph, that owner John Holst will frequently show his guests, is a 1934 picture of the unsmiling faces of Longino Mora, his fifth wife Clara and his 25th child, Carmina. Oddly, the photograph also portrays a woman behind the counter standing before a mirror who is smiling broadly. The woman is not reflected in the mirror she stands in front of. Might this be the mysterious Eva?

The most popular rooms are the Best Gals' Room, which was converted from the cribs of the "most popular soiled doves" during the brothel's heyday. Another well liked guest suite is Big Bertha's Room that was created from three of the original cribs and accommodates up to four persons.

YUMA

Hotel Lee

Figure 39: The Hotel Lee

The Hotel Lee is Yuma's oldest hotel. It was completed in 1917 and is listed on the National Register of Historic Places. Located on a corner of what was once the busy Main Street of Yuma at the southern terminus of the commercial district, the building with its simple planes, applied ornaments and arches is an early simplified version of the Spanish Colonial

Revival which was to become a major trend in western architecture during the 1920's and 30's.

The Hotel Lee, named for Robert E. Lee and the southern "Ocean to Ocean" Lee Highway, has been renovated and restored. The lobby and rooms offer the ambiance of the Victorian era with Victorian antiques and historic memorabilia throughout the hotel[21].

Along with the famous southern charm for which the Hotel Lee has been noted, there are also several ghosts who call this historic old hotel home. At least three spirits have been seen by guests and employees of the Hotel Lee. One of these ghosts is that of a young teenage girl that is usually seen late in the evening carrying towels down the back hall.

Another of the ghosts is believed to be the original owner of the Hotel. She is normally seen walking the halls late at night and has been known to knock on or rattle the doors of the rooms. The third spirit is that of an Indian woman believed to pre date the hotel. She has been seen hovering above the guests beds and is known to take small screwdrivers and awls belonging to the maintenance staff only return them by hiding them in odd places.

---

[21] http://www.hotellee.com/

COLORADO

ALMA

The Schwartz Hotel

People have reported seeing strange lights and experiencing an eerie feeling as they walk by the Schwartz Hotel. Legend states that a father and son had a dispute during the 1800's and shot each other. They are now believed to haunt the place. They even frightened one lady so horribly that she hanged herself from the upper balcony. Witnesses have claimed to see her in the upstairs hallway.

ASPEN

Aspen is the largest city and county seat of Pitkin County, Colorado. According to 2006 Census Bureau estimates, the population of the city is 5,804. Founded as a mining camp in the Colorado Silver Boom and named because of the abundance of aspen trees in the area, the city is now a ski resort and cultural center.

Hotel Jerome

The Hotel Jerome is located at 330 E. Main Street. Though you check for a peaceful visit, you may find that it is anything but peaceful. Ever find a lost, shivering and soaking wet boy in your hotel room? Well you might at the Hotel Jerome. A woman recently found just that in Room 310 of the Hotel Jerome. When a staff member arrived to help, the boy had vanished, leaving only wet footprints. At that time, no children were registered in the hotel.

Legend has it that a child had drowned in the hotel's original swimming pool. Room 310 is located right in the middle of an addition to the hotel that was built over that original pool.

BLACKHAWK

The historic City of Black Hawk is a Home Rule Municipality in Gilpin County, Colorado, United States. The city population was 118 at U.S. Census 2000, making Black Hawk the least populous city in Colorado. The tiny city is a historic mining settlement founded in 1859 during the Pike's Peak Gold Rush. It is located adjacent to Central City, another historic mining settlement in Gregory Gulch. The two cities form the federally designated Central City/Black Hawk National Historic District.

The area flourished during the mining boom of the late 19th century following the construction of mills and a railroad link to Golden. The town declined during the 20th century, but has been revived in recent years after the 1991 establishment of casino gambling following a statewide initiative in 1990.

Gilpin Hotel & Casino

The original Gilpin Hotel in Blackhawk dates back to the late 1800's when the Central City/Blackhawk area was known as the richest square mile on earth. Back in those days, the hotel also housed a one-room school upstairs, with a teacher by the name of Lucille Malone. Lucille was in love with an area miner and was devastated when her lover was run over by a wagon in front of the hotel. Unable to deal with her grief, the distraught schoolteacher threw herself over the balcony of the hotel dying in the very same street as her former lover. However, Lucille seemingly remains at the hotel according to several guests. Manager Randy Reker is positive he saw a woman entering a second-floor room. When he approached the room, no one was there. He's sure it was Lucille Malone, who jumped from the building to her death a century ago, when she learned her lover was run over by a wagon in front of the hotel. One of the casino's restaurants bears her name.

Lucille also does more than just roam the building. One former employee believes that she warned him of a fire in the building. Before the advent of gambling in Blackhawk, the Gilpin Hotel was just a small town hotel catering to tourists and people living within the area. A man by the name of Thomas was staying there with a girlfriend in the early 1990's. His girlfriend, who was a bartender at the hotel, lived in one of the upstairs rooms. The old hotel was a little run down at the time and Thomas stated that the only way to turn out the light in the bathroom was to twist the bulb.

Before retiring for the evening, he unscrewed the bathroom light and climbed into bed. However, at some point during the night, the light mysteriously turned back on. Getting up to unscrew the bulb again, Thomas was startled by a clatter from the first floor – the sound of pots and pans dropping from the wall. Fearing an intruder, he grabbed a baseball bat and crept down the stairwell, only to find the kitchen fully engulfed in flames.

Thomas raised an alarm and the eight to ten guests quickly began to evacuate the hotel. Thomas returned to the hotel, covering his nose with a sock to retrieve one person who had collapsed from smoke inhalation. Unfortunately, one guest returned to the hotel to get some papers, never to come out again.

Thomas is convinced that Lucille provided a warning when the mysterious light bulb turned back on in the middle of the night. After the fire, the hotel was refurbished and today it is the Gilpin Hotel and Casino. Employees and guests still report sightings of the ghostly Lucille.

Cold spots are common, as well as occasional power outages. The story among employees goes that once the security guards were watching the cameras upstairs, as usual, when they spotted a small girl holding a balloon. They radioed other security guards, alerting them that a minor was in the building (which is illegal), and the guards searched for her. One was even seen on the video to be right next to the girl, but he couldn't see her. She could be seen on the camera, but not "in person". Eventually the girl disappeared.

BOULDER

The City of Boulder (40°1'N, 105°16'W, Mountain Time Zone) is a home rule municipality located in Boulder County, Colorado, United States. Boulder is the 11th most populous city in the State of Colorado and the most populous city and the county seat of Boulder County. The United States Census Bureau estimates that in 2005 the population of the City of Boulder was 91,685, the population of the Boulder Metropolitan Statistical Area was 280,440 (161st most populous MSA), the population of the Denver-Aurora-Boulder Combined Statistical Area was 2,869,377 (15th most populous CSA), and the population of the Front Range Urban Corridor was 3,965,289.

Boulder is the home of the University of Colorado at Boulder, the largest university in Colorado, Rivendell College, a private liberal arts college and Naropa University, the only accredited Buddhist-inspired university in the United States. Boulder's elevation is 5,430 feet (1,655 m) and it is 35 miles (60 km) northwest of Denver.

College Inn

The College Inn is a building circa 1970, which is currently used as a conference center/hotel, though in recent years it has also served as a dormitory. It is said to be haunted by at least one entity of unknown origin. The building director of eight years knows of no death in the building during his time here. The activity centers on the third floor, particularly the south side of the building. Phenomena range from rummaging sounds coming from bathrooms, elevator doors opening and closing when people walk by, smoke-like apparitions, reddish stains appearing on walls and voices that have been heard by nearly every staff member. There is a globe style lamp in the hallway that leads to the bathroom in every unit of the hotel. One night in July of 1999 every single one fell to the floor while the hotel was between conferences and vacant, it took two days to put them back up.

Lumber Baron Inn -

In the 1970's this house was converted into apartments. A young run away girl, 17 years old, lived in one apartment. She was raped and murdered one night. A friend of hers stumbled upon the murder and was also killed. The house is now a bed and breakfast. There have been several haunting incidences, including a sighting of a girl in a flapper dress. Footsteps have been heard and seen on the squeaky steps.

CANON CITY

Cañon City was founded in 1859 during the Pikes Peak Gold Rush as a commercial center for miners. In 1862, A. M. Cassaday drilled for petroleum six miles north of town, near an oil seep. He struck oil at a depth of 50 feet, and completed the first commercial oil well west of the

Mississippi. He drilled five or six more wells nearby, and refined kerosene and fuel oil from the petroleum, and sold the products in Denver. A number of ore smelters were built in Cañon City following the discovery of gold at Cripple Creek in 1891.

St. Cloud Hotel

The St. Cloud Hotel is no longer in operation at the time of this writing, since the owners both got into some serious trouble with the law. This hotel is the most mysterious, wonderful hotel with a lot of historical value. The St. Cloud is located in the center of old mining settlements where there were gunfights and much emotional excitement. The original owner built the hotel just south of Canon City in a small town that was to be the state capitol building before Colorado became a state, this town is called Silvercliff.

The man who built the hotel got into trouble when he refused to pay taxes. There was a gunfight over the whole deal but somehow he managed to keep his hotel but had to move it to Canon City, CO. They moved it brick by brick (numbered of course) to Canon City, and put it back together. Guests of the hotel have reported seeing strange figures wandering the halls. These spirits are never unsettling, just a bit surprising. There have also been a number of complaints of a young child playing with her ball in the halls of the hotel and disappearing potpourri.

The St. Cloud Ghosts enjoy playing games, hiding things from the housekeepers and turning off lights and televisions, stacking furniture and startling guests and employees, the St. Cloud Hotel is both charming and spooky.

CENTRAL CITY

The town of Central City is an old mining town located near Denver, with many very well preserved buildings, including a historic opera house/theatre. Central City in Colorado although inhabited by the living was well spoken of for its vaporous inhabitants (one really can't say deceased when the specter doesn't themselves admit to it). In a certain bar on the main street on the floor there is a lovely painting of a woman, it is carefully maintained by the proprietor.

Founded in 1859, Central City quickly acquired the reputation of being in the middle of "the richest square mile on earth." As many as 30,000 miners flooded the area in search of their fortunes but by the end of its second year, most of the placer gold was gone and hard rock mining began. The settlement's population ebbed and flowed with the building of new mines and survived through the 1870's and 1880's.

The tale is that a distraught miner painted it when his wife died of consumption[22]. He went into the bar and drank himself into a stupor, while stupefied he proceeded to paint his wife's portrait on the floor. He spoke tenderly of her sweetness almost as an incantation to give it the life she lost so young. He painted long into the night and on to past noon. Once it was complete he slept, he never awoke. They buried him next to her and some say on the anniversary of his death you can hear them talking tenderly to each other through her portrait on the dance floor.

However, by the early 1900's Central City was becoming a virtual "ghost" as buildings were dismantled – the lumber and materials shipped to more thriving settlements. By the 1920's the settlement had only about 500 residents. Struggling along as tourist town for years afterwards, the town regained some prosperity with the passing of legalized gambling in 1991. However, the nearby town of Blackhawk, nearer to the highway, benefited most from the new law and Central City continued to struggle along. However, the benefit to Central City is that most of its historic buildings remain

---

[22] See The Teller House below.

intact. Central City, although inhabited by the living, is also said to remain home to a number of lingering spirits.

Teller House

This historic building is one of the few that survived the 1874 Central City fire. Built at a cost of $84,000 in 1872, the owners spent an additional $20,000 for furnishings, making it the finest hotel (outside of Denver) west of the Mississippi. In the beginning, the rate for this luxury hotel was 50 cents per night plus an additional $2.50 tariff. President Grant visited Central City and the Teller House in 1873 and again in 1876. For his 1873 visit, a path of silver ingots valued at $12,000 was laid from his carriage to the front door of the hotel as a "welcome mat."

This building houses the famous and mysterious "Face on the Barroom Floor" painting, done by Herndon Davis in 1934. This lovely painting is carefully maintained today. Legend has it that the woman's likeness was painted by a distraught miner when his wife died of consumption. As the story goes, the miner drank himself into a stupor and then proceeded to paint his wife's portrait on the floor. Speaking tenderly of her, he painted long into the night and on to past noon. Once the artist was finished, he slept, never to wake again. Buried next to his beloved wife, witnesses say that on the anniversary of his death, the couple can be heard talking tenderly to each other through her portrait on the floor.

COLORADO SPRINGS

Colorado Springs was founded in August 1871 by General William Palmer, with the intention of creating a high quality resort community, and was soon nicknamed "Little London" because of the many English tourists who came. Nearby Pikes Peak and the Garden of the Gods made the city's location a natural.

Within two years his flagship resort the Antlers Hotel opened, welcoming U.S. and international travelers as well as health-savvy individuals seeking the high altitude and dry climate, and Palmer's visions of a thriving, quality resort town were coming true. Soon after, he founded the Denver & Rio Grande Railroad, a critical regional railroad. He maintained his presence in the city's early days by making many grants or sales of land to many important civic institutions in the community. Palmer and his wife saw Colorado Springs develop into one of the most popular travel destinations in the late 1800s United States.

The town of Palmer Lake and a geographic feature called the Palmer Divide (and other more minor features) are named after him, and a bronze sculpture of Palmer on a horse with one leg raised (denoting being seriously wounded in a battle that later caused his death), is prominently displayed downtown in front of Palmer High School, the center of a busy intersection.

Black Forest Inn:

This place is not really in Colorado Springs but in Black Forest. The Black Forest Inn, so the story goes, used to be a family home and there was a couple that lived there. The wife had a secret lover who wanted her to run away with him. The two argued about her refusal to leave her husband and in a fit of anger her "lover" killed her and then, in a nearby barn, he killed himself. There are actual cold spots and weird happenings that go on there."

Broadmoor Hotel

The Broadmoor Hotel was built in 1891 and converted to a Casino in 1918. Always a man of taste, flamboyant Spencer Penrose was the guiding force behind the modern incarnation of the Broadmoor. An entrepreneur from Philadelphia who made big bucks trading mining claims in Cripple Creek, Colo., Penrose in 1918 transformed what was a casino and small hotel into a larger, 250-room hotel. He sought to bring the opulence and luxury found in European hotels to the Colorado Springs foothills. Thanks to renovations and additions, the Broadmoor now has 700 rooms.

According to local legend, most of the hauntings stem from a deadly fire that once swept through the hotel. Guests have claimed to hear the ghosts of the fire victims running and screaming.

Days Inn - Airport –

There is an older gentleman that haunts room 207 at the Days Inn-Airport. There have been reports of cold spots, curtains opening and closing and "thumping" when no other guests are present. Hotel staff knows about him and the housekeepers don't like to clean that room without at least two others nearby.

Cascade Blvd. - Hearthstone Inn –

There have been reports of visitors to the Hearthstone Inn on Cascade Boulevard seeing a little girl run through the houses laughing. Some witness have experienced cold spots in the houses that would give you goose bumps and things flying of hooks on the walls and shelves. No reports of anyone that ever felt threatened but there have been claims of witnesses that they were so scared that their hearts stopped on several occasions.

Rock Ledge Ranch —

The Rock Ledge Ranch was once a hospital for Tuberculosis patients in the 1800s. Lights turn on by themselves; footsteps can be heard in the upper levels. The antique rocking chair in the basement moves by itself.

CRIPPLE CREEK

At an elevation of 9,494 feet and just below timberline, for many years Cripple Creek's high valley was considered no more important than a cattle pasture. Many prospectors avoided the area after the misnamed Mount Pisgah hoax, a mini gold rush caused by salting (adding gold to worthless rock).

In 1891, however, rich ore was found and the last great Colorado gold rush was on. Thousands of prospectors flocked to the region, and before long W. S. Stratton located the famous Independence lode, one of the largest gold strikes in history. By 1900 Cripple Creek and its sister city, Victor, were substantial communities.

During the 1890s, many of the miners in the Cripple Creek area joined a miners' union, the Western Federation of Miners (WFM). A significant strike took place in 1894, marking one of the few times in history that a sitting governor called out the National Guard to protect miners from forces under the control of the mine owners.

By 1903 the allegiance of the state government had shifted, however, and Governor James Peabody sent the Colorado National Guard into Cripple Creek with the goal of destroying union power in the gold camps. The WFM strike of 1903 and the governor's response precipitated the Colorado Labor Wars, a struggle that took many lives.

Through 2005, the Cripple Creek district produced about 23.5 million troy ounces (731 tonnes) of gold. The old underground mines are exhausted, but open pit mining has operated since 1994 east of Cripple Creek, near its sister city of Victor, Colorado.

With many empty storefronts and picturesque homes, Cripple Creek once drew interest as a ghost town. At one point the population dropped to a few hundred, although Cripple Creek was never entirely deserted. In the 1970s and 1980s travelers on photo safari might find themselves in a beautiful decaying historic town. A few restaurants and bars catered to tourists who could drive by weathered empty homes with lace curtains still hanging in broken windows.

Colorado voters allowed Cripple Creek to establish legalized gambling in the early 1990s. Cripple Creek has a population of around 1500 residents and is currently more of a gambling and tourist town than a ghost town. Casinos now occupy many historic buildings. Casino gambling has been successful in bringing revenue and vitality back into the area.

Imperial Hotel & Casino –

Workers report it is guaranteed that visitors to the Imperial Hotel & Casino will see or hear something that wasn't of this world. Some people say they have seen a man falling down the stairs, or a young lady walking by during a mellow drama wearing clothing from the 1800's. A former employee worked at the casino for three years has documented some of what happened while they were there at - Not a Ghost of a Chance

Palace Hotel & Casino –

Visitors to the Palace Hotel & Casino report feeling a gentle nudge as they walk down the stairs.

DENVER

Denver was founded during the Pikes Peak Gold Rush in the Kansas Territory in 1858. That summer, a group of gold prospectors from Lawrence, Kansas arrived and established Montana City on the banks of the South

Platte River. This was the first settlement in what was later to become the city of Denver. The site faded quickly, however, and was abandoned in favor of Auraria (named after the gold-mining town of Auraria, Georgia) and St. Charles City by the summer of 1859. The Montana City site is now Grant-Frontier Park and includes mining equipment and a log cabin replica.

On November 22, 1858, General William Larimer, a land speculator from eastern Kansas, placed cottonwood logs to stake a claim on the hill overlooking the confluence of the South Platte River and Cherry Creek, across the creek from the existing mining settlement of Auraria. Larimer named the town site Denver City to curry favor with Kansas Territorial Governor James W. Denver. Larimer hoped that the town's name would help make it the county seat of Arapaho County, but ironically Governor Denver had already resigned from office. The location was accessible to existing trails and was across the South Platte River from the site of seasonal encampments of the Cheyenne and Arapaho.

The site of these first towns is now the site of Confluence Park in downtown Denver. Larimer, along with associates in the St. Charles City Land Company, sold parcels in the town to merchants and miners, with the intention of creating a major city that would cater to new emigrants. Denver City was a frontier town, with an economy based on servicing local miners with gambling, saloons, livestock and goods trading. In the early years, land parcels were often traded for grubstakes or gambled away by miners in Auraria.

The Colorado Territory was created on February 28, 1861, Arapahoe County was formed on November 1, 1861, and Denver City was incorporated on November 7, 1861. Denver City served as the Arapahoe County Seat from 1861 until consolidation in 1902. In 1865, Denver City became the Territorial Capital. With its new-found importance, Denver City shortened its name to just Denver. On August 1, 1876, Denver became the State Capital when Colorado was admitted to the Union.

Between the years of 1880 and 1895 the city experienced a huge rise in city corruption, as crime bosses, such as Soapy Smith, worked side-by-side with elected officials and the police to control the elections, gambling, and the bunko gangs. In 1887, the precursor to the international charity United Way was formed in Denver by local religious leaders who raised funds and coordinated various charities to help Denver's poor. By 1890, Denver had grown to be the second largest city west of Omaha, but by 1900 it had dropped to third place behind San Francisco and Los Angeles.

In 1901 the Colorado General Assembly voted to split Arapahoe County into three parts: a new consolidated City and County of Denver, a new Adams County, and the remainder of the Arapahoe County to be renamed South Arapahoe County. A ruling by the Colorado Supreme Court, subsequent legislation, and a referendum delayed the creation of the City and County of Denver until 1902-11-15. Denver hosted the 1908 Democratic National Convention to promote the city's status on the national political and socio-economic stage.

Denver was selected to host the 1976 Winter Olympics to coincide with Colorado's centennial celebration, but Colorado voters struck down ballot initiatives allocating public funds to pay for the high costs of the games, so the games were moved to Innsbruck, Austria. The infamy of becoming the only city ever to decline to host an Olympiad after being selected has made subsequent bids difficult. The movement against hosting the games was based largely on environmental issues and was led by then State Representative Richard Lamm. Lamm was subsequently elected as Colorado governor in 1974.

Beat icon Neal Cassady was raised on Larimer Street in Denver, and a portion of Jack Kerouac's beat masterpiece On the Road takes place in the city, and is based on the beat's actual experiences in Denver during a road trip. Beat poet Allen Ginsberg lived for a time in a basement apartment on Grant Street (no longer standing), and Kerouac briefly owned a home in the Denver suburb of Lakewood in the late spring and summer of 1949. In addition, Ginsberg helped found the "Jack Kerouac School of Disembodied Poetics at Naropa," in nearby Boulder at the Buddhist College Naropa University, then Naropa Institute.

Denver has also been known historically as the Queen City of the Plains because of its important role in the agricultural industry of the plains regions along the foothills of the Colorado Front Range. Other nicknames that Denver has had include The Rail City, for the city's importance as a North American rail hub, and Capital of the Rocky Mountain Empire, for the city's pre-eminence in the Rocky Mountain region. Several US Navy ships have been named USS Denver in honor of the city.

Brown Palace Hotel –

The Brown Palace Hotel is located at 321 Seventeenth Street. While it is known as being one of the most noted hotels in the city, it is also known for being one of the most haunted hotels in the city.

The Brown Palace is so luxurious you'll wish you could spend an eternity here. As it happens, some of the guests have. When one thinks about all the people who have walked the halls and dined at the tables of The Brown Palace Hotel during the past century, it seems only natural to assume that a few "spirits" may have lingered behind. Could there be a more sublime place to spend an eternity than within the beauty of this triangular-shaped, architectural gem?

In truth, The Brown Palace's ghosts are few, and none seem to represent those who played strong roles in its life. None of the apparitions claim to have met Henry Brown, the founder and builder, or Augusta Tabor who lived in the hotel for a few unhappy years following her divorce from the Silver King. Although the "Unsinkable" Molly Brown took singing lessons in Room 629 while she was in Denver, there have been no haunting melodies emerge from within its walls since then.

But there have been ghostly encounters and sightings of spirits that illustrate mortal life in an urban hotel, giving us a glimpse of the people and events throughout the last 100 years.

- In the boiler room of this historic old hotel, witnesses recount the sounds of babies crying. Others tell of unexplainable cold drafts. There is also a void on the wall of the boiler room that leads to unexplored tunnels.

- There are commonly reports of feminine laughter and chatter in the eighth-floor hallway outside present-day Room 804, which was originally part of the ballroom. One supposes these to be Victorian young ladies, enroute to powder their noses, giggling about the eligible men who'd escorted them to the ball.

- Once, a bellman delivering morning newspapers to upper-floor rooms found some of the papers stolen from his cart. A few minutes later, he encountered an apparition dressed in an old-fashioned uniform. He was so frightened that he quit the next day.

- Recent sightings by hotel employees have also involved a spirit in uniform. He has been seen outside The Brown Palace Club dressed in his "conductor's uniform." The hotel originally housed the ticket office for the Rock Island Railroad, so it seems plausible that a mortal conductor might have once walked these halls. When sighted, this spirit merely disappears through the wall.

- A maintenance man was recently called to Room 523, in which the guest complained that the room was too hot. He was met at the door by a pale, old woman wearing a long, black flowing gown, who responded to his question about the problem. When he'd adjusted the controls, he turned to tell her that everything should be fine, and she was nowhere to be seen. He called the front desk to report that the job was complete, and asked if they could let the guest know when she returned. There was a long pause before the desk clerk answered, "That room is unoccupied."

- A telephone operator had two encounters with an unseen wraith. Twice, when she took off her coat to hang it in the closet, she turned from the door and felt something tugging at her skirt. Believing she'd caught it in the door as she closed it, she turned back to free it. The door was tightly shut and her skirt was not restrained by it. Other operators have reported seeing a woman in an old-fashioned pink formal walk through their space and disappear into the wall. A man in Victorian evening clothes made the same passage at other times.

- Prior to the main dining room being renamed Ellyngton's, this restaurant space was known as the San Marco Room, home to big bands and later, the San Marco Strings. One evening, a houseman went to investigate sounds coming from the dining room. Upon entering, he discovered a quartet of formally dressed musicians practicing their music. The houseman was not amused, as it was long past closing time. "You're not supposed to be in here," he said. They replied, "Oh, don't worry about us. We live here."

- Room 831 has a resident spirit who likes to sit upon the couch and cause doorstops to fly out from beneath the door jam.

- But the most sophisticated prank was played by the ghost of the woman who lived and died in Room 904. Mrs. Crawford Hill (Louise) was the undisputed queen of Denver society. Her glamorous life story ended with heartbreak and resulted in her living the last 15 years of her life in Suite 904. While conducting a "lovers and scandals" tour of the hotel, the historian began with Louise's story. After these new tours first began, the switchboard was inundated with calls from Room 904. When answered, there was only static on the line. How could this be happening? An extensive renovation was underway on the 9th floor, and her old apartment had been stripped of furniture, carpeting, wallpaper, lights, wires — and telephones. When Mrs. Hill's saga was dropped from subsequent tours, the calls ceased.

The Grosvenor Arms Apartments[23] -

The historic Grosvenor Arms Apartments located at 333 E. 16th Ave. anchors the corner of East 16th Avenue and Logan Street like a great battleship, its bricks and stones built for heavy service, still seaworthy after nearly 75 years. Boilers churning, brass-gated elevators rising and falling, the building harbors its secrets and gathers fresh ones each time a new tenant moves in. When they say they don't build them like they used to, this is what they mean.

---

[23] SINCE 1931, DENVER RESIDENTS FROM ALL WALKS OF LIFE HAVE CALLED THE HISTORIC GROSVENOR ARMS APARTMENTS HOME - Author: Laura Watt, Denver Post Staff Writer

The Grosvenor Arms Apartments opened for business in the fall of 1931. With its deep flagstone courtyard, medieval gray stone walls and winged serpents guarding the Gothic front door, coming here is like stepping into the past.

But it is very much in the present. Unlike many buildings of this vintage, the Grosvenor has survived and thrived virtually intact, without falling into seediness or disrepute, its 106 units still spiffy, full of character and sought-after.

In a rental market where the vacancy rate runs upward of 13 percent, the Grosvenor's is less than 5 percent, and its lobby and hallways teem with residents, many under 30.

"It's an extremely nice place to come home to," says 22-year-old Jesse Marks, a dancer with the Colorado Ballet. "It's beautiful, it's old. It's a nice mix of downtown residents."

Laura Paisley, a 25-year-old occupational therapist who has decorated her apartment in a spare, modern style, says the building felt like home to her when she moved in.

"I could tell that people were proud of this building," she says.

They were and are.

The reason The Grosvenor feels like home is because Louis Mack, the mogul who built it, wanted it that way, and because his daughter, 90-year-old Barbara Mack McKay, has insisted it stay that way. Although she has not lived in the building for years, she maintains her apartment on the seventh floor and comes often to see "her building."

"This is a family affair. It's my heritage," says McKay, who visited the site with her father every day when the building was going up. "My father felt people wanted privacy. That's why he used the best materials. It was built to be their home."

When it opened, the "absolutely fireproof" building was touted as having "the very latest" in modern conveniences: "The women folk will love the Eureka gas ranges" an article in The Denver Post said at the time.

The Eureka ranges are long gone, but original tile remains in most bathrooms, and the apartments retain the arched doorways, original woodwork, hardwood floors, telephone nooks and glass doorknobs popular in the '30s.

Thick, solid walls keep the noise to a muffle. All of the apartments are either one-bedroom or studios, so the Grosvenor was never for families with children. In fact, children were banned at the beginning, though not now. Today, one teenager lives in the building.

"In the early days, you had to have references to get in," said Andrew Caron, who has lived here with his wife for 30 years. "People were lawyers, doctors, professionals."

Current residents may skew toward high-tech office workers, but at least two denizens of The Grosvenor seem to come from the mists of time.

Ghosts - The Man in the Mirror and The Woman Upstairs

"Who knows what secrets these old buildings have?" says Marshall Gregory, who has lived at the Grosvenor for 10 years. "I do believe in ghosts. I don't discount (the stories) at all."

Gregory hasn't seen one, but others have. Janice Eldridge, who was resident manager at The Grosvenor for several years, twice saw a tall, broad-shouldered man dressed in a dark suit and fedora in one of the large mirrors that flank the lobby. He was looking at her.

"I said 'hello,'" she says.

Eldridge also felt the presence of an unseen young woman in the hallway outside the eighth-floor laundry.

"She had a very long skirt that would swish. Very elegant. I was never scared. I never felt a menacing feeling. I always felt like they were protecting us."

Teresa Montano, a weekend manager, also saw the man in the mirror, heard silverware banging in her kitchen sink in the middle of the night and once a very bright light flashed between her and a friend in the elevator after the friend accidentally flicked off the overhead light. Then there are the stories about the Woman Upstairs

"When your arms are full of laundry, she'll push the elevator button for you," Montano says.

The ancient Otis elevators, with their brass accordion doors, are notoriously fickle, often skipping floors or stopping between them. Lots of residents have some tale about something a little odd at The Grosvenor.

"I had a friend here leave for the weekend and when she came home her TV was on, on a sports channel. And she never watches sports," says Neil Sarno, a 32-year-old engineer for Douglas County. "

The storage units creep a lot of people out. There is definitely a certain presence and a spirit here." Ah, the storage units. Crypt-like, dimly lit, on the top floor, nobody likes going there, especially alone. They're chilly even when it's hot.

Eight floors down, in the office where it's not spooky at all, property manager Dick Pfeifer smiles gently when ghosts are mentioned. He's never seen anything supernatural, he says, and he's been running things at The Grosvenor for 25 years.

"I take care of business," he says. "What's special about this place? See that door? It's original. See that carpet there? It's in great shape."

It does seem a little strange, though, that when a visitor takes the elevator alone for the first time, she pushes Five and it takes her up to Eight - the haunt of The Woman Upstairs. The elevator pauses as if deciding, then eases back down and stops dead between Three and Four.

Another firm push on the Five button, and the old Otis rises slowly, reluctantly, to its intended destination.

Hearthstone Inn -

The Hearthstone Inn is comprised of two Victorian mansions. Constructed in 1885, the original building of the Inn is listed on the National Register of Historic Places. It was built as the home of the Judson Moss Bemis family - great philanthropists for the city of Colorado Springs and for the Colorado College. The second mansion was built in 1900 and later used as a tuberculosis boarding house. Both buildings were thoughtfully renovated to become the Hearthstone Inn, operating since 1978.

The Hearthstone Inn, the Bemis Brother Bag Company, the Fine Arts Center and the Taylor Museum,

Bemis Hall, Taylor Hall, the Cogswell Theatre at Colorado College and the Colorado Springs Day Nursery are all examples of businesses and benefactions connected by one family - that of Judson Moss Bemis.

Mr. Bemis brought his family to Colorado Springs from the Boston area in 1881, in hopes that the climate would suit his wife - Alice Cogswell Bemis - and ease her throat ailment. More than ca century later, our community is all the better for the contributions the Bemis family has made to Colorado Springs.

Judson M. Bemis was a pioneer in many ways. He moved his family out west when Colorado was still a state in its infancy. Colorado Springs itself had been settled for less than a decade when Mr. Bemis decided to build his family a home on North Cascade Avenue.

Early photographs of the house, completed in 1885, show it looming large with nothing in sight between the house and the mountains to the west. Mr. Bemis had the house built like others at the time - with larger windows facing east to bring in the cool morning air, and smaller windows on the west since that air was considered stale and less healthy. With his family settled in, Mr. Bemis could tend to his other priority, the Bemis Brother Bag Company.

In 1858, Mr. Bemis conceived the idea of using cotton bags to package flour rather than wooden barrels, which had been the norm. With a small investment and virtually no education, he started the Bemis Brother Bag Company in St. Louis. A pioneer in the packaging industry, Mr. Bemis' small company grew to include locations in the U.S., Mexico, Canada, and Europe.

His visits to Colorado Springs were rare, since he was so busy working at his business. But his contributions to the young City, as well as those of his wife and daughter, Alice Bemis Taylor, were tremendous. Mr. Bemis was a trustee of Colorado College from 1912-1918. He gave the college $100,000 to build Bemis Hall, a dormitory built in 1908. He gave the college a grant to establish the Department of Business Administration and Banking in 1914. Only General Palmer and William S. Jackson has given as much to Colorado College as the Bemis family.

Mrs. Alice Cogswell Bemis was also a great benefactor to the city. In 1897, she established the Colorado Springs Day Nursery, a day care operation for children of tubercular mothers. In 1923, her daughter, Alice Bemis Taylor, built a permanent facility for the Day Nursery at South Tejon and Rio Grande streets, where it still stands today. Mrs. Bemis also gave land and funds to the YMCA to build a gymnasium. She established the first Woman's Club in Colorado Springs and began the Wednesday Art Club in 1885, where women gathered each week to discuss the arts.

Alice Bemis Taylor followed in her parents' footsteps with the legacy she left behind. The Fine Arts Center, with the Taylor Museum, was established in 1936, through the generous donations of Mrs. Taylor and based on her own collection of Native American arts. Taylor Hall, a dining hall at Colorado College was built in 1956 through her donation. She also donated the organ to Grace Episcopal Church where she began the Taylor Concert series, in honor of her late husband, Frederick M.P. Taylor.

The Bemis family left its indelible mark on Colorado Springs, representing the pioneer spirit and the spirit of giving back to the community. The Bemis family home, now on the National Register of Historic Places, was the original building of the Hearthstone Inn. Pioneers of a different kind established this bed and breakfast. The original owners, Dot Williams and Ruth Williams, bought the Bemis family home in 1977, which by then had become a rundown apartment building. They restored the building back to its original grandeur and opened the doors for guests in 1978. The Hearthstone Inn was one of the first bed and breakfast hotels in Colorado Springs - Dot and Ruth were forerunners in this aspect of the hospitality industry.

Judson Moss Bemis was generous with his fortune, and his family followed suit, giving back to the community in which they lived. The Hearthstone Inn itself takes its place as a gift to our community in a number of ways -- by preserving the important history of the Bemis family and its connection to Colorado Springs, by maintaining a fine example of late 19th century architecture and style, and by opening its doors to guests worldwide to experience and enjoy the Victorian splendor that the Bemis family began.

It would seem that the members of the Bemis family are so concerned about their former home that some of them return to keep an eye on thing. The Hearthstone Inn suffered through a severe lightning storm in 1999. In the days after the storm, two separate guests requested relocation from the same room on the third floor of the north house. The first guest gave no reason. However, the second said she saw a picture of a woman with piercing blue eyes hanging on the wall. The eyes were so piercing that she removed the picture. The next day, a custodian discovered a mirror face down on the floor, leaving to question whose reflection was in the mirror.

Lumber Baron Inn:

At the turn-of-the-century, John Mouat amassed his fortune in lumber and built this 8,500 sq. ft. mansion from a combination of woods including cherry, oak, maple, poplar, sycamore, and walnut.

Current owner Walter Keller and his 6-year-old son, John, give a tour of the Lumber Baron Inn at 2555 W. 37th Ave. The Valentine Room was where the bodies of Cara Knoche and Marianne Weaver were found in 1970.

Johnny Keller walks down the creaky staircase. His mother once heard the stairs make noise and saw the steps move, but no one was there. Johnny also shares his bedroom with a spirit he calls Nicey Nice Ghost because, 'Every morning he says hello.'

Walter Keller was barely of legal drinking age on April Fool's Day 1991 when the newlywed sunk his heart and all his money into the dilapidated north Denver mansion. Where neighbors saw a fright house with boarded-up windows, drooping eaves, cracked paint, rotted wood and overgrown weeds, Keller envisioned a romantic bed and breakfast filled with turn-of-the-century antiques.

Before opening the Lumber Baron Inn, the former teacher says he knew nothing about neighborhood lore that dubbed his Victorian home haunted.

"I knew there had been two murders here," says Keller, "but that's all."

Then, not long after move-in day, he watched from the porch as a group of preteens planted themselves on the sidewalk and eyeballed him and his 10,000-square-foot house.

"All of the sudden one of them ran up to the side of the house, tapped the wall, then they all ran down the block screaming," recalls the 34-year-old Keller, while seated in the bed and breakfast on a claw-foot Empire love seat with angels carved into the mahogany.

He named his inn after Scottish timber mogul John Mouat, who built the house in 1890. Keller says the restoration has attracted historic-preservation awards along with a parade of couples wishing to wed in the Lumber Baron's Victorian garden and sleep in its neoclassical Honeymoon Suite.

Since snapping up the "fixer-upper" for $80,000 in 1991, Keller has invested more than a dozen times that amount restoring the house to its original charm. That's why the homeowner was up late one night in 1993 cutting shower tiles when he had an eerie encounter.

Keller crouched just between the Honeymoon Suite and the Valentine Suite, where crushed velvet adorned a king-size Indonesian wedding bed. The house was quiet, but something bothered him.

"I just felt something," Keller says. "It was like someone was standing over me, watching. Then I'd look over my shoulder, and no one was there."

The presence vanished in a frozen gust, and the hairs rose on his neck. Keller says it's no coincidence that the encounter happened just outside the Valentine Suite. Thirty-three years ago, the room was the scene of a gruesome double homicide.

It seems that the house had a violent past. In 1970, Keller's dream home was a run-down apartment house. Cara Lee Knoche, a free-spirited 17-year-old with flaxen hair and a bumpy nose like her dad's, had abandoned her suburban upbringing to live in a $48-a-month studio there.

"*I remember going up that stairwell,*" says Jack Isenhart, head of security at Regis University and a former Denver police detective. "*It was dank and mysterious, and there was this pungent odor of marijuana.*"

Marianne Weaver an 18 year old friend often dropped by Knoche's apartment. The night of Monday, Oct. 12, 1970, the Arapahoe Community College student left her Lakewood home intent on another visit.

According to newspaper reports the following day, a friend drove past Knoche's hangout pad in the middle of the night. He spotted Weaver's car and found it odd that Knoche's apartment was dark.

The man later told police that he parked his car and walked inside. He found Knoche's door ajar. When the friend flicked on the light, he discovered Weaver with a bullet hole in the middle of her forehead. Her killer had positioned her body on Knoche's bed with arms crossed over her chest, vampire-style.

Looking closer, the witness spotted another arm sticking out from under the bed. Knoche had been stripped, strangled and packed away like an empty suitcase. The witness fled the house and called police from an all-night diner on Federal Boulevard.

"There's something awful.... There's two dead girls there," he said.

Police spent months interviewing neighbors and friends of the victims.

"There were a lot of people in and out of there," says Isenhart, one of the first investigators on the scene 33 years ago. "Remember, this was a time when people traveled the streets and were often taken in by friends. We had some good suspects, but they never panned out. I think

we even had one guy try to confess to the crime, but his story didn't fit."

Police never uncovered a murder weapon or a motive - something that haunts Isenhart to this today.

"*You just don't forget something like that, the way those girls were murdered*," he says. "*There's always been a mystique surrounding that house.*"

Now the unsolved murders are part of the Denver Police DNA Cold Case Project. Mitch Morrissey, chief deputy district attorney in charge of the project and someone who's familiar with the Lumber Baron Inn killings, says Denver police are reviewing cold cases using updated technology and FBI grant money.

"*I can't tell you any specifics because this is still an open case*," Morrissey says. "*But generally what we look for in old homicides is hair, body fluids, fingernail clippings or old clothing that might have blood on it.*"

The fact that the murders were never solved may be why the spirits of Cara Lee Knoche and Marianne Weaver are restless, according to Dee Chandler, a certified paranormal investigator.

Chandler co-founded the Mile High Paranormal Society. She also has conducted haunted tours of Lower

Downtown and is negotiating the rights to a story about communicating with another Denver murder victim.

The former attorney says Marianne Weaver is the ghost who most often appears to people at the Lumber Baron Inn.

"The other girl (Knoche) was a runaway who had a lot of guests in and out of her apartment," Chandler says. *"But Marianne's death was unexpected. She was in college. She was a noted horsewoman. Now she's yelling out for her crime to be solved."*

During the initial investigation, police suspected Weaver's murder was unplanned. Chandler agrees.

"When you pose somebody the way she was laid out, it means 'I didn't mean to kill you, you just happened to witness this and I can't have a witness,'" she says. So perhaps it was Weaver who brushed past Walter Keller in 1993, and who also appeared to Keller's ex-wife, Maureen Welch, a couple of years later.

Welch stayed up late waiting for guests to arrive. The woman sat alone in her foyer, reading, just below a creaky stairwell.

"Suddenly she heard someone coming downstairs," Keller says as he guides a visitor through the house. He steps heavily to show the loose, whiny planks in his

staircase. *"When she stood up and turned around, she could actually see the wood move, but no one was there."*

On another occasion, the mother of a bride planning to wed at the Lumber Baron was arranging floral centerpieces in the inn's fourth-story banquet hall.

"Out of the corner of her eye she saw a young woman in a blue flapper dress sitting on the window bench with a glass of champagne in her hand," Keller says while glancing around a turreted sunroom just off the banquet hall.

"When she walked back to say hello, she felt a cool blast of air, and there was no one there. She literally ran down the stairs, screaming for me."

Ghost hunt launches

Tales like these prompted Chandler to conduct a ghost hunt at the Lumber Baron Inn three years ago. The event, which she chronicles in "Ghosthunt: A Guide to Ghost Photography and Field Investigations" (Great Unpublished, $15), happened on the 30th anniversary of the double homicide.

That night, dozens of people poked around the house attempting to capture spirits on film. Even the overnight guests were in the mood to be spooked.

"*I encourage cynicism,*" Chandler says. "*But everybody experienced something that night, and they all reported it individually.*"

Chandler could relate to their experiences. That night, she stood alone in the banquet hall when an invisible someone whispered in her ear. She was also with a group of people in the kitchen when the refrigerator suddenly shifted back and forth. While sensing a presence in one the guest bathrooms, Chandler snapped what she says is a photo of Weaver's reflection in a mirror hung 8 feet off the floor.

The ghost hunt convinced Chandler that the two murdered girls are not the only spirits at the Lumber Baron Inn.

"*There's a black woman who was apparently a maid who died in the house,*" she says. "*The General stands on the second-story guarding the entrance, and the mischievous 1930s flapper girl is usually upstairs.*"

Both Chandler and Keller discovered the General after smelling pipe smoke throughout the house, which is a nonsmoking facility. Other people reported smelling women's powder.

Children are most in tune with ghosts, Chandler says. Perhaps that's why Keller's 6-year-old son, Johnny, shares his bedroom with one.

"*Yes, yes. I see him every day,*" says the first-grader. "*I think he's a boy ... a teenager. He looks kind of gray. He has orange eyes and a yellow nose.*"

Johnny calls this spirit Nicey Nice Ghost because "*Every morning he says hello.*"

When the boy gets older, he may learn from his dad that a police psychic also once walked through the basement where Johnny's room is now and insisted she felt a presence there. Right now, Dad doesn't worry much about scaring his son. "What's fun is that even when we're alone," Keller says, "we never feel alone[24]."

Oxford Hotel:

The Oxford Hotel is Denver's oldest hotel. It was built in the 1880's during the silver boom by brewer Adolph Zang. Mr. Zang operated the largest brewery in Colorado and hired architect Frank E. Edlbrooke to design a grand hotel. The Rocky Mountain News at the time commented on the Oxford's gadgets and Gilded Age opulence when it opened on October 3, 1890.

---

[24] SOURCE: The Denver Post, October 19, 2003, Elana Jefferson, *Invisible roomers never complain, Ghosts make themselves at home, say Lumber Baron Inn owners*

Famous guests of the Oxford have included Presidents Truman and Clinton, Colorado Governor Stephen L.R. McNichols and his brother Denver Mayor William H. McNichols Jr. (the namesake of the former home of the Denver Nuggets and Colorado Avalanche sports teams). Labor leaders such as Mother Jones and Big Bill Haywood stayed at the Oxford, where authorities tried to imprison her and thugs beat him up for daring to defy Colorado's powerful mine owners.

The historic Oxford Hotel, Denver Colorado, provides a sophisticated hideaway in the midst of Denver's lively LoDo district. A member of Historic Hotels of America and listed on the National Register of Historic Places, this downtown Denver hotel has played a central part in the city's colorful past since 1891. It is also among the list of haunted hotels in Denver.

- One alleged paranormal sighting comes from a hotel worker who cleans the downstairs ladies bathroom late at night and has found pennies on the floor. Supposedly, the pennies mysteriously fall from the ceiling in that bathroom.

- Another comes from a caterer who was setting up for a ballroom banquet. The caterer walked by the ballroom and saw 4 men playing cards and smoking cigars. He backed up to have another look and they were gone.

- Up on the third floor of the Oxford, there have been sightings of a woman in a white dress and reports of voices arguing in a hotel room. Years ago, the room was the scene of a murder involving a jealous husband and his wife.

- On another occasion, a businessman who was a frequent guest, went to the front desk one night and told the front desk associate, "You have a ghost." His story was that he'd just brushed his teeth to climb into bed for the night. Once in bed, he was startled to see the bathroom light snap on by itself, the bathroom door opened, the sheets on the other side of the bed pulled back and he suddenly felt a presence in the bed next to him.

  Even though he was unnerved, he told whatever "It" was that he was ok with sharing the bed. The sheets pulled back into place, the bathroom light went off and the door quietly closed back to where it was.

- Of all the Oxford's ghosts, the most memorable is the late poet Thomas Hornsby Ferril, whose words and spilled drinks still haunt the Oxford. Lisa Johnson, the Cruise Room's legendary mixologist, can point out where Ferril sat with his Wasted Friday Afternoon Club, a group dedicated to fighting the Protestant work ethic. Whenever Ferril lacked funds, he'd quietly let it out that it was his birthday. Then he gratefully, humbly accepted drinks, dinners and birthday cake.

  On one occasion, which really was his birthday, the Oxford's interior reverberated with the hee-hawing of his present--a jackass.

Windsor Hotel

The Windsor Hotel was known as the hotel of the upper crust and high class because only formal dress was allowed in the salons and dining rooms, the Windsor Hotel at 18th and Larimer fell to the wrecking ball in 1960. There is an interesting historical tale that goes with this.

When Henry Brown and his wife moved to Colorado his first intention was to move onto California with his wife and try to strike it rich in the mines. When he walked into the Windsor in his western clothes to get a meal he was rudely turned away because he was considered a member of the common people. He was so offended that he decided to buy some land and build his own hotel that catered to the common man and allowed casual wear for dining. He swore that his new hotel, The Brown Palace, would outlast the Windsor and sure enough to this day his hotel is thriving while the Windsor is now just a memory. Henry Brown's picture is in the statehouse and he is the only non-elected official in that area of the capitol building. Why? Because he donated the land the building stands on.

As for ghosts in the Windsor it is said that the spirit of Mr. Tabor (once a very wealthy owner of several silver mines in Leadville) and Baby Doe, "the most beautiful woman in Colorado" still linger in the area. Mr. Tabor spent many nights there with Baby Doe, his mistress and later second wife, rather than go home to his first wife Augusta. When Tabor's fortune evaporated with the silver crash of the early 1890's he kept a room in the Windsor where he died in poverty in 1899. Baby Doe then left Denver to live 36 long lonely years in a small cabin on the grounds of the Matchless Mine in Leadville Colorado. She died in the cold of winter and was discovered some months later in the spring on the floor of the cabin. It was soon after that her ghost was seen at the Windsor and some say can still be seen at the site where the hotel once stood.

DURANGO

The town was organized in September 1880 by the Denver and Rio Grande Railroad to serve the San Juan mining district. The D&RG chose a site south of Animas City for its depot after Animas City refused to pay a "dowry" to the D&RG. The city is named after Durango, Mexico. The word Durango originates from the Basque word "Urango" meaning "water town".

Strater Hotel

According to the owner of the Strater Hotel he has had many people leave the hotel in "the middle of the night" when they have encountered spirits in the hallway.

Maids have also reported seeing people enter unoccupied rooms and upon entering to assist the customer, the maids find the room empty.

Jarvis Suites

The Jarvis Suites, located on 10th and Main Avenue in Durango was built in 1888. It is now on the National Register of Historic Places. The Jarvis Suites is a charming hotel. Ghost hunters had conducted investigations in a few of the rooms there, but they soon found that Room 208 provided them with the voices of a man and woman. On one investigation, they had their motion detector set up. After setting up the equipment, they had left the room for a bit of course, locking the room.

The motion detector went off while they were not in the room. While listening to their cassette, they noticed a woman's voice right after they turned it off. So, when booking a reservation at the Jarvis Suites, tell them you want Room 208. The ghosts there probably won't keep you up too late!

The Rochester Hotel

The Rochester Hotel, located at 726 East Second Ave., was a low-class apartment building for most of its existence. When its owners began renovating the hotel in

1994, contractors and workers refused to come back to finish their jobs.

"They just ended up quitting," said Kirk Komick, co-owner of the Rochester Hotel and The Leland House. "They didn't feel comfortable there."

Since the renovations were completed, Komick said he receives reports about twice a year about a ghost in the hotel's "John Wayne Room," Room 204. Guests always see a woman standing in the bedroom, either wearing elaborate Victorian dress or classy lingerie. About twice a year, guests in Room 204 of a local hotel report seeing a woman with dark hair wearing Victorian clothing – or very little clothing at all.

EMPIRE

Empire is a town in Clear Creek County, Colorado. The population was 355 at the 2000 census. The town is a former mining settlement that flourished during the Colorado Silver Boom in the late 19th century. It is located in the valley Clear Creek west of Denver, on the north side of the valley. The town consists of several commercial establishments and residents. U.S. Highway 40 passes through the town as its ascends towards Berthoud Pass, putting the town on the direct route between Denver and Middle Park.

The Pratt Hotel

The Pratt Bed and Breakfast was built in the late 19th century and is haunted by the first owner's daughter, Millie Pratt, who fell down the very steep front stairway. She only seems to appear to women. Her room is the one by the top of the stairs. She whispers "mother!" in women's' ears at night and several have seen her fall down the stairs or lying at the bottom of the staircase.

ESTES PARK

Estes Park is a town in Larimer County, Colorado on the Big Thompson River. The population was 5,413 at the 2000 census. As of a 2005 census estimate, the population has risen to 5,812. The town is named after Joel Estes, who founded Estes Park in 1859. The town is a popular summer resort and headquarters for Rocky Mountain National Park.

The town's outskirts include The Stanley Hotel. Once a fine example of Edwardian opulence the 1906 building once had Stephen King as a guest. His stay at the

Stanley inspired him to change the locale for his novel, *The Shining*, from an amusement park to the Stanley's fictional stand-in, the Overlook Hotel. Estes Park is also recognized as the birthplace of the American credit union movement.

Trail Ridge Road, the highest continuous highway in the United States, runs from Estes Park westward through Rocky Mountain National Park, reaching Grand Lake over the continental divide.

The town suffered severe damage in July 1982 from flooding caused by the failure of Lawn Lake Dam.

Baldpate Inn

The Baldpate Inn, built in 1917, consists of a main lodge with 12 guest rooms and restaurant, 4 charming cabins which have been recently renovated, a homestead residence, outbuildings for staff housing and storage, horse barn, and 12.86 acres of forested land with sweeping mountain views.

Gordon and Ethel Mace built this charming lodge in 1917, and it stayed in their family until 1986 when the family lost ownership of it. Of course this did not deter Ethel, however, who has haunted her old room for years. She especially likes to sit in a wing-backed rocker before a fireplace in what is now a storage room, her feet up, reading the Bible. Gordon hates smoking. Few guests are able to keep a cigarette lit for long - something smashes it out or steals the pack! Ethel must be somewhat of a prohibitionist, because mixed drinks seem to spill and fly off tables fairly often.

The Stanley Hotel

You may have heard of an author by the name of Stephen King. And you may have heard of a book and film called "The Shining." Here lies the inspiration within...

The Stanley Hotel began construction in 1906 and opened in 1909. F. O. Stanley and his wife Flora built their home nearby and then this hotel. F.O. built a hydroelectric plant up in the mountains so as the hotel could be all electric. He even had phones in every room. Both were quite a luxury at the time.

The Stanley was a summer resort so heat was not added until 1979. Before then, any heat in the building came from fireplaces on the first floor. Other than that, it is mostly the same as in 1909.

Besides a history that includes the last quarter of the film "Dumb and Dumber," many celebrities and tourists have enjoyed the Stanley over the years. Most notably was author Stephen King, who wrote half of "the Shining" in room 217. Stephen King came back when the recent ABC mini-series was filmed here as well. Stanley Kubrick's film version was NOT filmed here. They used sets for most of that film.

There aren't any known evil spirits at the Stanley Hotel. The Shining was fiction after all. The ghosts of the owners are still around. In the music room, Mrs. Stanley's favorite, you may hear the piano playing by itself. Or you may feel the presence of Mr. F.O. Stanley around the lobby or in his favorite space, the Billiard room.

The fourth floor is the old servant quarters and fairly active with spirits. You will notice the narrow corridors. The sound of children playing in the halls is common even when there isn't a child in the building. The center of the activity in the hotel seems to be the very active room 418.

In addition to its regular guests, the hotel is also said to play host to a number of other worldly visitors. The most notable is F.O. Stanley himself who is most often seen in the lobby and the Billiard Room, which was his favorite room when he was still alive. On one such occasion, he was said to have appeared during a tour group's visit to the Billiard Room, materializing behind a member of the tour. Bartenders at the old hotel also report having seen F.O. stroll through the bar, disappearing when they try to cut him off at the kitchen.

Not to be left out, Flora Stanley also haunts the hotel, continuing to entertain guests with her piano playing in the ballroom.

Employees and guests have reported hearing music coming from the room, and when they take a peek into the room they can see the piano keys moving. However, as soon as someone walks across the thresh-hold to investigate further, the music stops and no more movement can be seen upon the keys of the piano.

There are several rooms in the hotel that seem to be particularly haunted. One is Room 407, which is said to sometimes be occupied by Lord Dunraven, who owned the land prior to F.O. Stanley[25]. Reportedly, he likes to stand in the corner of the room near the bathroom door. On one such account, witnesses reported that a light in that corner kept turning on and off. While the light was off, they told the ghost that they knew that he was there, they would only be staying two nights, and would he please turn the light back on. The light turned back on. However, later when the lights were turned off and they were trying to sleep, noises were constantly heard from the nearby elevator during a time when the elevator was not in use. At other times, a

---

[25] He was, of course, run out of town after trying to swindle folks out of their land and money.

ghost has been reported to be looking out the window of Room 407, when the room is not booked.

Room 418 gets the most reports of haunting activity apparently from children's spirits. Cleaning crews report having heard many strange noises from the room, as well as seeing impressions on the bed when the room has been empty. When guests stay in the room, they often report that they hear children playing in the hallway at night. One couple reportedly checked out of the hotel very early in the morning, complaining that the children in the hallway kept them up all night. However, there were no children booked in the hotel at the time.

There have also been many reports by guests of haunting activities in Rooms 217 and 401.

Tour guides tell a story of the ghost of a small child who has been seen by many of the staff in various areas of the old hotel. Reportedly, Steven King also saw the child, who was calling out to his nanny on the second floor. Other past employees report footsteps and apparitions seen throughout the building.

A visitor reported that a group of people spent the night up at the Stanley Hotel in Room 418. It definitely proved to be a hot spot for spirits. They took have over 100 photos of orbs, and there was a medium encounter in the

Dining Hall, and a hair raising encounter about 2am in Room 418. After these incidents, the visitor that made the report called it a night and quickly headed out of there.

This huge, eerie hotel built in the early 1900's was a resort for famous celebrities and such. Past employees have mentioned hearing footsteps and seeing various apparitions. A ghost has been spotted in room 407 in the window and most other guests complain about hauntings in Room 217 and 401.

EVERGREEN

Homesteader Thomas Bergen arrived in 1859, establishing a ranch and stage stop north of present-day downtown Evergreen. Bergen's Ranch was recognized as a settled area at the establishment of Jefferson County, Jefferson Territory. Subsequent settlers homesteaded south of Bergen along Bear Creek Canyon and the downtown area grew around the confluence of Cub Creek and Bear Creek. Fellow homesteader Dwight P. Wilmot is credited with naming the area "Evergreen"; his home has been preserved and still functions as a private residence across the street from his namesake Wilmot Elementary School.

The town grew on the lumber demand for buildings in Denver and by the 1880s, the town could boast a population of 200 people and six operating sawmills. Improvement of the road from Denver up Bear Creek Canyon in 1911 and electrical service reaching the town in 1917 spurred further growth and the town became a popular summer destination for Denver residents. Resorts like Troutdale-in-the-Pines, Greystone Guest Ranch and the Brook Forest Inn opened and entertained Denverites and celebrities including film stars of the day and Presidents Franklin D. Roosevelt and Theodore Roosevelt, who both vacationed at the Troutdale. In the 1950s, improved utilities in town and the rising popularity of automobiles began to entice more future residents to stay year-round and the town became known as a commuter community.

Brook Forest Inn

The Brook Forest Inn is a beautiful mountain Inn with numerous ghost stories. The Inn is haunted on the top floor by two ghosts: Jessica, a chambermaid murdered by her lover, a stable hand, and the stable hand who committed suicide after killing her. Cold presences are felt going the stairs to the third floor, according to the staff.

The Second floor is said to have been the location that "Carl" murdered his wife after finding out she had an affair with another man. (The AFSPR and RMPRS investigated and found numerous magnetic anomalies in the suggested room for the past homicide.) The third floor is said to hold the spirit of a mischievous little boy who died from the flu or some other type of illness. It is said he can be heard running up and down the hallway late at night. The surrounding forest is believed to be haunted by the Indians that lived there hundreds of years ago.

FAIRPLAY

Fairplay is a town in Park County, Colorado. At an altitude of 9,953 ft. (3,034 m), it is the fifth-highest incorporated place in the state of Colorado. The population was 610 at the 2000 census. It is the county seat of Park County. A historic gold mining settlement, the town was founded in 1859 during the early days of the Colorado Gold Rush. It is the largest community in the grassland basin of Colorado known as South Park, sitting on the west edge of the basin at the junction of U.S. Highway 285 and Colorado State Highway 9. It is on a hillside just east of the Middle Fork South Platte River, near where Highway 9 ascends the river valley northward to Alma and Hoosier Pass. It is a quiet town, and the roads surrounding it have a low volume of traffic. Although it was founded during the initial placer mining boom, the mines in the area continued to produce gold and silver ore for many decades up through the middle of the 20th century.

The town consists of modern retail businesses along the highway, as well as a historic town on the bluff above the river along Front Street. The northern extension of Front Street along the river has been preserved and has become the site of relocated historic structures as an open air museum called South Park City, intended to recreate the early days of the Colorado Gold Rush. Most of the residences in town are located on the hillside east of Colorado State Highway 9, in the vicinity of the schools and Park County Courthouse. The majority of the streets in town were finally paved in 2005.

The town of Fairplay, Colorado is the basis for the town of South Park, Colorado in the television series South Park.

Fairplay Hotel

Many people today believe that the Fairplay Hotel is haunted by a woman's ghost who harks back to days gone by. Affectionately known as 'Julia', she returns to the hotel every year in late October, drawn by her memories of dancing upon the hotel's wooden floors during the town's annual Harvest Dance.

Sometimes, after a late night residents have reported sightings of 'Julia', as well as claiming to have heard music on the dance floor accompanied by rhythmic creaking of the planks, as though 'Julia' was again dancing under a harvest moon.

Hand Hotel

In the small town of Fairplay, the historic Hand Hotel, bordered by dirt streets and filled with century-old furniture, is home, still, to Grandma Hand. Grandma, it is said, likes her room just as she left it. Once, when a guest tried to take a nap in his (Grandma's) room, he kept hearing a woman's voice asking for her rocking chair. After searching other rooms, he brought back a rocking chair and the voice was stilled.

The ghost of a dark mastiff has been seen repeatedly at the Hand Hotel. One guest saw and felt the dog pull the bed covers off her. When she tried to re-cover herself, the dog bared its teeth and disappeared. Five years ago, a young boy was attacked by the mastiff as he and his father were building a haunted house for Halloween in the hotel's basement. Former hotel owner Pat Pocius confirmed dog bites on the boy's hand, as did a doctor.

FLORENCE

Florence is a city in Fremont County, Colorado, USA. The population was 3,653 at the 2000 census. Florence contains ADX Florence, one of two federal supermax prisons in the United States.

Florence Hotel

According to local legend, there was a man who took a woman and her baby into the basement of the Florence Hotel and buried them in the basement floor, covering the grave with cement. People have seen the lady walking down to the basement and also in the bathrooms, bedrooms and the old dining room. At night some people can hear the baby crying, if you ever go there (ask to sleep in the pink room.)

FORT COLLINS

Fort Collins was founded as a military outpost of the United States Army in 1864. It succeeded a previous encampment, known as Camp Collins, on the Cache La Poudre River, near present-day Laporte. Camp Collins was erected during the Indian wars of the mid-1860s to protect the Overland mail route that been recently relocated through the region. Travelers crossing the county on the

Overland Trail would camp there, but a flood destroyed it in June 1864. Afterward, the commander of the fort wrote to the commandant of Fort Laramie in southeast Wyoming, Colonel William O. Collins, suggesting that a site several miles further down the Poudre would make a good location for the fort. The post was manned originally by two companies of the 11th Ohio Volunteer Cavalry and never had walls.

Helmshire Inn

On the third floor of the Helshire Inn a worker claims ghosts would undo their work after rooms had been tidied lot of times the curtains would be open again, one time a bed had been "unmade" and toilets would flush when nobody was on the floor with me. Also, the basement, in certain areas, seems to have a presence, it may not be the same one from the third floor. You should give Fort Collins another glance since this area was an intense battleground. Look back in some of the old newspapers. Especially areas near and around Legacy Park and Martinez Park.

Holiday Inn Holidome

There's a ghost of a man in the top hall of the northwest wing of the Holiday Inn Holidome that is an ominous presence. The ghost of a woman looks out over the swimming pool, from one of the rooms, when children are playing, supposedly to watch over them. The main apparition though, is of a little girl who haunts a room across the hall and a bit east of the now unused king suite. She does little poltergeist activities mainly- (guests there often find their key cards missing, etcetera) and she also blasts the air conditioning.

GLENWOOD SPRINGS

Glenwood Springs has a long, interesting history. Its unique location at the confluence of the Colorado River and the Roaring Fork River as well gaining a stop on the railroad historically made it a center of commerce in the area. The city has seen numerous famous visitors including President Teddy Roosevelt who spent an entire summer vacation living out of the historic Hotel Colorado. Doc Holliday, a wild west legend from the O.K. Coral gunfight, spent the final months of his life in Glenwood Springs and is buried in the town's original cemetery above Bennett Avenue.

Hotel Colorado

The Hotel Colorado in Glenwood Springs, a favorite retreat of Teddy Roosevelt, takes its ghost stories in stride. It's not unusual for guests to report having seen a little girl in the hallways, bouncing a red ball, even though no children were staying in the hotel. Each report of her sighting over the years describes similarities; the girl never ages, her clothing never changes. Also, some guests hear running footsteps of many people coming directly at them. When it seems the thundering herd will run them over, the sounds disappear.

One guest reported that on one occasion that she stayed at the Hotel Colorado that she stayed up a real long time. Feeling restless, she went downstairs and saw and heard the piano keys moving up then down. She just knew it had to be a ghost! Then she smelled smoke. When she went back to her room, she saw and heard a ball bouncing. She didn't know if it was the little girl, or just her imagination.

One night while talking in the bar at the hotel a naval officer and a physician discovered that they were seeing the same nurse. They became so incensed at her two-timing that instead of going after each other, they both bludgeoned her to death in room 454. They tried to hide the body in the freight elevator but were discovered. They were encouraged to leave town quietly (which they did) and she was buried in Glenwood's cemetery along with Doc Holliday.

Subsequent guests who stayed in room 454 were awakened to screams and yells and found a woman's bloody body. This happened so often that the Hotel Colorado converted the room to a storage closet. However it did not end there as out in the hallway you can still smell her Gardenia scented perfume. She's only one of the ghosts that creep around the halls of the Hotel Colorado which offers special nighttime ghost tours during which you may get a glimpse of Al Capone, Legs Diamond, Theodore Roosevelt, and his original Teddy Bear which is supposedly a token of a bear the President shot on a hunting trip to Glenwood Springs.

The History of Hotel Colorado is a magical journey through time, from the late 1800s to the new millennium; the timeless secrets of a rich century are unlocked within the pages of this beautifully illustrated, hard cover book. Presidents, silver barons, debutantes, society's elite, movie stars and romantics have graced this Grand Dame's hallways each leaving an indelible footprint for us to forever remember. What began as a simple historical record became a five-year labor of research, writing, and love. Each upturned stone opened the door to ten additional enduring pieces of heritage. These pages capture the highlights.

Historic Hospitality

In 1893, Hotel Colorado arrived on the scene during a thrilling time in the history of America's West. With its European fashioned spa, the resort surfaced onto a land of prosperity; to serve the wealthy, to house the ailing, to offer a playground to society's elite. The Hotel Colorado's originator, Walter Devereux, spared no expense in the creation of the "Grande Dame." Situated in the existing lounge, a sheet of water twelve-feet broad dropped in a waterfall a distance of twenty-five feet from the rear-wall rim to a pool beneath. Guests could sit beside the pool in the early morning catching trout enough for their breakfast.

The south court, the current courtyard, had a large pool in its center from which an electrically lit fountain shot a jet of water 185 feet high into the air, making an iridescent rainbow spray against the sunlight.

Diamond Jack Alterie

During the roaring '20s, Hotel Colorado became an attractive playground for Chicago gangsters such as the Verain Brothers, Bert and Jack (alias Diamond Jack

Alterie). Armed in gun belts, Diamond Jack Alterie wore flashy diamonds in rings, shirt studs, watches, and belt buckles. Cloaked in bodyguards, these big spenders arrived at the Hotel Colorado via large Lincoln convertibles.

The Unsinkable Molly Brown

Rising quickly to wealth as a result of her husband's abundant gold strike, Molly Brown visited the Hotel Colorado to enjoy one of society's favorite playgrounds. Today, one of the Hotel's Tower Suites has been transformed into a living tribute to this dynamic woman of history. The Molly Brown Suite is magnificently appointed with family photos, memorabilia, and period furnishings.

Doc Holliday

In May, 1887 a tuberculosis-filled gambler with a reputation for violence rode into Glenwood Springs. John H. "Doc" Holliday, thirty-five-years-old and deceitfully charming, managed to have strength to play for gambling houses even though battling for his life. Though his visit preceded the existing Hotel Colorado, his therapy at the Hot Springs forever links him to the historic beginnings of the hotel. When he died on November 8, 1887, his employers took up a collection to pay for his grave... the second grave in the Linwood Cemetery. A marker still memorializes him and his involvement with Wyatt Earp at the legendary shoot-out at the O.K. Corral.

Presidents

Many presidents have visited the Hotel Colorado. On September 23, 1909, President William Howard Taft arrived in his private train car. He was presented with wild raspberries and mountain trout for breakfast and shown the vapor baths and pool. A parade of carriages carried Taft and his party to Hotel Colorado. When offered exclusive use of the Hot Springs pool, he declined saying, "I've found it's much better for a man of my size not to bathe in public." After being presented with raspberries and mountain trout for breakfast, he spoke to 700 people from the Hotel's "Roosevelt" balcony.

The ghosts do not seem to care about the splendor and the important people around them. They just go on with their day to day activities. Doors open and close by themselves, elevator goes up and down by itself, smell of cigar smoke fills the air even when no one is smoking in lobby, a little girl in a Victorian dress is often seen playing on the staircase, and a murdered chambermaid appears at night in the Devereux Room.

LEADVILLE

Placer gold was discovered in California Gulch on 1860, during the Pikes Peak Gold Rush, and the town of Oro City sprung up near present-day Leadville. The boom was brief, however, and Oro City never became a major settlement. The placer gold mining was hampered by heavy brown sand in the sluice boxes.

In 1874, gold miners at Oro City discovered that the heavy sand that impeded their gold recovery was the lead mineral cerussite, that carried a high content of silver. Prospectors followed the cerussite to its source, and by 1876, had discovered several lode silver-lead deposits. The city of Leadville was founded near to the new silver deposits in 1877, setting off the Colorado Silver Boom. By 1880, Leadville was one of the world's largest silver camps, with a population of over 40,000.

In 1882, the Tabor Opera House hosted Oscar Wilde on his lecture tour of the West, one of many celebrities who graced the city. Mayor David H. Dougan invited Wilde to tour the Matchless silver mine and open their new lode: "The Oscar." Wilde later recounted a visit to a local saloon, "where I saw the only rational method of art criticism I have ever come across. Over the piano was printed a notice - 'Please do not shoot the pianist. He is doing his best.'"

In its early years, Leadville was the site of some famous mining swindles. When the Little Pittsburg mine exhausted its rich ore body, the managers sold off their shares while hiding the real condition of the mine from other stockholders. "Chicken Bill" Lovell dumped a wheelbarrow of rich silver ore into a barren pit on his Chrysolite mining claim in order to sell the claim to Horace Tabor for a large price; but Tabor had the last laugh when his miners dug down a few feet farther and discovered a rich ore body. Later, the manager of the Chrysolite mine fooled an outside mining engineer into overestimating the ore reserves of that mine.

Leadville in the 1950'sThe city's fortunes declined with the repeal of the Sherman Silver Purchase Act in 1893, although afterwards there was another small gold boom. Mining companies came to rely increasingly on income from the lead and zinc.

The district is credited with producing over 2.9 million ounces of gold, 240 million ounces of silver, 1 million short tons of lead, 785 thousand short tons of zinc, and 53 thousand short tons of copper.

During World War II, Leadville was a popular spot for visits by soldiers at nearby Camp Hale, but only after the town acted to curb prostitution; until then, the United States Army declared the town off-limits for its personnel. The war also caused an increase in the mining of molybdenum at the nearby Climax mine. At one point the mine produced 75 percent of the world's molybdenum.

Downtown Leadville June 2005The closing of the Climax mine in the 1980s was a major blow to the town's economy. In addition, the many years of mining left behind substantial contamination of the soil and water, so that the Environmental Protection Agency designated some former mining sites in Leadville as Superfund sites. The town is now 98% cleaned up and the Superfund designation is about to expire. The town has made major efforts to improve its economy by encouraging tourism and emphasizing its history and opportunities for outdoor recreation.

The National Mining Museum and Hall of Fame opened in 1987 with a federal charter. The town is the site of the Leadville Trail 100 series of races and other events for runners and mountain bicyclists. Leadville is known for its festive atmosphere. Local celebrations include Boomdays in early August (a tribute to the city's mining past) as well as the Crystal Carnival late each winter featuring a skijoring competition on Harrison Avenue. As a center for such celebrations, Leadville has unofficially been labeled "Parade Capital U.S.A." in recognition of the frequent, though sometimes small parades held in the downtown area.

Alps Motel

Visitors to the Alps Motel have reported experiencing drastic temperate changes in some of the rooms as well as feelings of dread or that something was wanting to cause you harm.

Delaware Hotel

In the old rough-and-ready mining town of Leadville, the Delaware Hotel is a classic Victorian jewel - period antiques, crystal chandeliers, brass fixtures, and ghosts. During its heyday many famous people walked the streets of this historic mining town. These include; Doc Holiday, Houdini, John Phillips Souza, Butch Cassidy and "The Unsinkable Molly Brown", to name but a few.

The Delaware Hotel, known as the "Crown Jewel" of Leadville, has remained an active part in Leadville history and continues to represent the graciousness of the Victorian era. During one recent, warm summer, a painter, restoring one of the hotel's hallways, felt a frigid blast of air pass by him. He didn't wait for its return; he left his task unfinished. Perhaps, he experienced the spirit of Mary Coffey, who was shot in the back and paralyzed by her husband in their room at the hotel in 1889. Now, the vision of a woman haunts the Delaware, appearing only from the waist up.

06.13.03: Dane writes, "*Hi. I have an experience that I had at the Hotel Delaware in Leadville Colorado. I'm 18 now but this was way back when I was in 6th or 7th grade. My family went on a trip through Colorado for Spring Break. We stopped and stayed the night at the Delaware. That night my dad and I went exploring through the hotel. The staff never told us of the story of the "Lady in White". Well, we went different ways and I was walking down the hall and heard the chandeliers moving so I turned and look just in time to see the chandeliers swinging and a lady in white walk through a room door. My dad never did see anything until we were coming back together from dinner and as we walked up the stairs the lady in white was walking down and almost walked right into us but vanished about two feet in front of us. It was only until the next morning that we reported it to the desk that they told us the story of the lady in white. It frightened my dad and I but she was a beautiful woman that looked to be in her 30's."*

Abe Lee discovered gold at California Gulch in the 1860's. Hundreds of gold seekers rushed in and their camp (a short distance east of Harrison Avenue) became known as Oro City. As the placer gold that lay on top of the ground for the taking was depleted, Oro City was deserted and the scene was desolate.

Discovery of silver in 1877 signaled another rush to upper California Gulch. Oro City No. 2 quickly grew. The Denver and Rio Grande Railroad arrived in August, 1880. President Ulysses S. Grant and his party were among the first passengers. Leadville's population had stabilized at 25,000. (hardy souls lured by discovery of the rich silver-bearing carbonate of lead ores in the California Gulch)

In the mid 1880's three brothers, William F., George F. and John W. Callaway, Denver queens ware merchants, came to Leadville. The brothers established a branch of their business on lower Harrison Avenue. They built the two-story Callaway Block on the northeast corner of Sixth and Harrison (which later burned). In 1886 they erected the Delaware Hotel as a monument to their home state. John Callaway was proprietor. The Delaware Block was completed by October, 1886 at an estimated cost of $60,000. The sidewalk level was designed for stores both in front and on the Seventh Street side. The second and third walk-up floors had fifty handsomely furnished rooms suitable for offices and bedrooms. The building was fitted with steam heat, hot and cold water, gas lights, 6 bathrooms and a few closets.

Delaware architect, George King, came to Leadville in time to take an active part in the building boom that was sweeping the city. King obviously favored the French Mansard design, which until the late 1880's was popular in mining towns. King was also the architect for the plush Tabor Grand Hotel directly across the street.

Eventually William and George returned to Denver and John remained to operate the Delaware Hotel. Historians note "the brothers retired from business in 1890 having made fortunes in legitimate business and investments.

Former Leadvillites, Dorthea and Arthur Hougland of Glenwood Springs recalled Callaway as a "delightful man who wore Benjamin Franklin glasses, a derby hat, and a vest with his suit. He had a phonograph and played classical music. Songs by Enrico Caruso were among his favorites." Mrs. Hougland spent much time as a young girl at the hotel. Her grandmother, Josephine Feller worked for Callaway.

Baby Doe Tabor, who became a tragic figure after Horace Tabor's death, lived alone at the Matchless Mine and often visited the hotel to warm herself. She would climb the front entrance stairs, walk to the office and seat herself at the desk where she would write letters. Baby Doe's feet were customarily wrapped in gunny sacks for warmth as she walked to town from her wooden shack at the Matchless Mine.

OURAY

Originally established by miners chasing silver and gold in the surrounding mountains, the town at one time boasted more horses and mules than people. Prospectors arrived in the area in 1875 searching for silver and gold. At the height of the mining, Ouray had more than 30 active mines. Yankee Boy Basin, located a few miles from town, boasts a beautiful spectacle called Twin Falls. Coors and Chevrolet have both used this beautiful location to shoot commercials. The town was incorporated in 2 October 1876, Ouray was named after Chief Ouray of the Utes, a Native American tribe. By 1877 Ouray had grown to over

1,000 in population and was named county seat of the newly formed Ouray County on 8 March 1877.

The Denver & Rio Grande Railway arrived in Ouray on 21 December 1887, it would stay until the automobile and trucks caused a decline in traffic, the last regularly scheduled passenger train was 14 September 1930. The line between Ouray and Ridgway was abandoned on 21 March 1953.

The Ouray County Courthouse, constructed in 1888.The entire town is registered as a National Historic District with most of the building dating back to the late 1800s. The Beaumont Hotel, Ouray City Hall, Ouray County Courthouse, St. Elmo Hotel, St. Joseph's Miners' Hospital (currently housing the Ouray County Historical Society and Museum), Western Hotel, and Wright's Opera House are all on the National Register of Historic Places.

In the fall of 1968 the film True Grit was filmed in Ouray County, including some scenes in the town of Ouray, most notably the Ouray County Court House.

In Ayn Rand's novel Atlas Shrugged, the protagonist's secret headquarters were in a beautiful valley in the Rocky Mountains called "Galt's Gulch". Galt's Gulch was inspired by Ouray, where Rand found inspiration to complete the novel, though she greatly expanded the small valley to include her many ideas for the story.

Beaumont Hotel

Newly and gorgeously renovated, the Beaumont Hotel is said to be haunted by the ghost of a young woman who was brutally raped and killed by one of the chefs working there. Apparently, he was never brought to justice over the murder and it is said that she occasionally has been seen on the balcony crying out because of the injustice. A woman reported that by chance she and her husband met up at the hotel with some friends. She said that as a child, she and her family had stayed in one of the upper rooms in the hotel, just before they closed it for so many years. Years later, when they had opened the Beaumont briefly for the local residents to tour, she found her way to that same room she had stayed in all those years before. She said no one went into the room with her. She took several pictures of the room. She took one photograph of an old picture hanging on the wall. When she got the pictures developed, there in that picture on the wall is the reflection of two men standing in old clothes. One has a scrolled up paper in one hand. They are standing as though talking to one another but stopping just in time to look toward her.

Local legend says that on a woman's wedding night she was brutally murdered by her new husband. So now she walks on every quarter of the moon at 2:15 a.m. all over the house in search of her husband. On the anniversary of her death you can see her being killed, but you can't ever see her husband just her, like she is dying by herself. Her husband stabs her twice in the chest and once in the leg. he then drug her down the service flight of stairs, where he proceeded to drag through the hallway and then hung her in a door frame, so don't ever go on the third floor by yourself.

Old Western Hotel

One of the oldest, still standing all wood hotels in the West is in Ouray. As with many old structures the world over, over the years the Old Western Hotel has been used for many purposes. While it was an art workshop, two lady artists saw, at different times, a lady on the staircase in old fashioned dress (1800s). They both drew or painted her picture and compared them. They were of the same woman. The employees say there are several rooms upstairs that are haunted. After closing up one night, they were sitting in the front lobby when they heard the cash register start operating in the adjoining bar.

St. Elmo Hotel

Several summers ago, at a 4th of July neighborhood picnic, an elderly lady in her 80s reported that one of the rooms in the St. Elmo Hotel is haunted by a woman. She said that the room number is 13 but that is debatable.

REDSTONE

Known as "the Ruby of the Rockies," Redstone was developed by turn-of-the-century industrialist John Cleveland Osgood whose coal empire spurred construction of the Crystal River Railroad and Redstone's historic dwellings. As an experiment in "enlightened paternalism," Osgood constructed 84 cottages and a 40 room inn, all with indoor plumbing and electricity for his coal miners and cokers, as well as modern bathhouse facilities, a club house with a library and a theatre, and a school. Most of these craftsmen-era Swiss style cottages are still used as homes in Redstone.

Osgood constructed "Cleveholm Manor," the opulent 42-room Tudor-style mansion now commonly referred to as "the Redstone Castle" for his second wife, Swedish Countess Alma Regina Shelgrem. By the time Cleveholm was completed in 1902, the estate included servants' quarters, a gamekeeper's lodge, a carriage house, and a greenhouse.

Despite Osgood's remarkable accomplishments, it was Alma who made the greatest impression on Redstone's early 20th Century inhabitants with her remarkable sense of noblesse oblige. Alma was known among the coal workers and their families as "Lady Bountiful" for her legendary generosity.

Redstone Inn

At the Redstone Inn, in the utopian mining community near Carbondale, a spirit inhabits the third floor. The staff has named him George and, from reports, he's a busy guy. There are sounds of furniture moving, doors opening, toilets flushing, and music coming from the attic. No housekeeper will go to the inn's third floor alone.

Redstone was founded by John Cleveland Osgood, an ambitious turn-of-the-century entrepreneur. Initially on a scouting mission for a railroad company, Osgood recognized the vast potential for developing a full scale coal mining operation in and around Redstone and throughout Colorado. Along with a handful of investors, he began building his mining empire. In 1892 he merged with an iron and steel manufacturing company in Pueblo to form the Colorado Fuel and Iron Company (CF&I).

The high-grade coking coal of the Coal Basin area, 4 1/2 miles west of Redstone, and the beehive coking ovens in Redstone itself, spurred the construction of the Crystal River Railroad. This rail line connected the coal mines up-valley to the main lines in Carbondale where the coke was then transported to the steel mills in Pueblo. By 1900 the mining operations at Coal Basin and Redstone were in full swing.

John Osgood did more than run a profitable mining enterprise. In order to improve the living conditions of the miners and as a social/industrial experiment, he constructed 84 Swiss chalet style homes in Redstone to house miners with families and an elegant 20 room inn (Now the Redstone Inn) for his bachelor employees, all of which featured indoor plumbing and electricity, a luxury for the times. Modern bathhouse facilities and a club house which included a theater and library where also provided.

Shortly thereafter, Osgood began construction of his private residence, the lavish Cleveholm Manor, a 42 room Tudor-style structure complete with servants quarters, guard and carriage houses.

It wasn't long before Osgood's mining company was taken over in a bitter stock war. The mines and coke ovens closed, and Osgood, a private man, who had mingled with the financial giants of the era and was considered one of America's six leading industrialists, disappeared from public view. In 1925 Osgood returned to Cleveholm with his third wife, Lucille. At that time he oversaw the complete renovation of the Inn and started what is now the historic Redstone Inn. A year later, he died, leaving Lucille his entire estate.

SILVERTON

The historic Town of Silverton is a Statutory Town that is the county seat of San Juan County, Colorado. Silverton is a former silver mining camp in the San Juan Mountains that is now a federally designated National Historic District. The town population was 531 at U.S. Census 2000.

Silverton is linked to Durango by the Durango and Silverton Narrow Gauge Railroad, a National Historic Landmark. Silverton no longer has active mining, but subsists by maintenance of US-550 (which runs from Montrose to Durango), mine pollution remediation, retired folks, and tourism.

Grand Imperial Hotel

Luigi Regalia had killed himself in Room 28 of the Grand Imperial Hotel on November 1, 1890. He had made an earlier attempt on his birthday on October 6, but his landlady came in on him before he could carry out the act.

On November 1 he put on his best suit of clothes, took a room at the Grand Imperial Hotel and wrote a letter to his friend Carlo Barsotti of New York. Later that evening he put a gun to his head. While holding a small mirror in front of his face, he pulled the trigger. The bullet slammed through his skull from above his right ear, blowing out the center of his forehead near the hairline, badly fracturing the cranium. Two doctors attempted to bring Luigi back from the brink, but he succumbed quickly... and has never left the hotel.

STERLING

Sterling is a city in Logan County, Colorado. According to 2006 Census Bureau estimates, the population of the city is 12,589. It is the county seat of Logan County. It is home to the Northeastern Junior College and the Sterling Correctional Facility.

Ramada Inn

It is known that if you enter room 104 of the Ramada Inn you can see a woman in a night gown with what looks to be a blood stain on the front where she was supposedly shot walks around the room cleaning.

TRINIDAD

Trinidad is city in Las Animas County, Colorado, United States. According to 2006 Census Bureau estimates, the population of the city is 9077. It is the county seat of Las Animas County.

Trinidad has been dubbed the "Sex Change Capital of the World", because a local doctor had an international reputation for his sex reassignment surgery. In the 1960s, Dr. Stanley Biber, a veteran surgeon returning from Korea, decided to move to Trinidad because he had heard that the town needed a surgeon.

In 1969 a local social worker asked him if he would perform the surgery for her, which he learned by consulting diagrams and a New York surgeon. Biber attained a reputation as a good surgeon at a time when very few doctors performed the operations. At his peak, Biber was performing roughly four sex change operations a day, and the term "taking a trip to Trinidad" became a euphemism for some seeking the procedures he offered. His surgical practice was taken over in 2003 by Marci Bowers.

Trinidad's reputation as the sex change capital has been uncomfortable for some residents, as it is otherwise a socially conservative small town. However, the revenue brought in by Biber was important to keeping the local hospital running, and Biber was himself a respected community leader. Biber was also featured in an episode of South Park where elementary school teacher Mr. Garrison undergoes a sex change operation.

Tarabino Inn

The Tarabino Inn is a historic Bed and Breakfast located in beautiful Trinidad, Colorado. Splendid antiques blended with modern conveniences pamper your senses and your soul. Tarabino Inn bed and breakfast lodging combines the elegance and way of life of the Victorian era with the comforting hospitality and atmosphere rarely encountered in today's world. Indulge in the old world warmth of antique furnishings, rich natural woodwork, Persian rugs, and much more...

One of the owners, Kevin discussed his background and the hauntings in this historic old building. He met his wife, Teresa, in the late '80's when he was working as a teacher in Elizabeth, Colorado, about an hour southeast of Denver. They soon moved to Seattle, but never considered it permanent, and spent numerous vacations studying the landscape and land prices throughout Colorado and the Southwest.

After remodeling and selling our home in Seattle, they flew to Santiago, Chile, where Teresa was born. They planned on looking for work teaching English, but instead got itchy feet and found ourselves wandering Latin America for over a year.

Upon their return, they took a road trip through Utah, Nevada, Arizona and New Mexico, but, once again, didn't stumble upon a town that "spoke to us." That is, until they came down Raton Pass and stopped in Trinidad. Teresa was ready to move there immediately. He started applying for jobs and was lucky enough to get hired as a school counselor for the local district.

Teresa and her sister saw the Tarabino House and loved it. The Tarabino Inn is now a limited liability corporation with four partners, his wife and himself, his sister-in-law, and her partner.

The first time Teresa and he were lounging on the front porch, two boys, maybe eight or ten years old, stopped in front of the house on their bikes and asked if the house was haunted. Apparently, the house had a reputation around town.

Their first big project was to tear off the roof and protect the structure with new roof and gutters. During that project, roofers asked about ghosts. We spoke with the former owner and, yes, he and others at the house had stories to tell. They even performed a ritual to drive the ghost into the basement coal bin (which doesn't seem like a very nice thing to do)!

Kevin reported that he has had numerous experiences personally, and others have as well, but stories of fright are rare. A few examples from his own experience: Twice he awoke to answer the call of nature and came across the image of a young woman in a nightgown. She was standing at the foot of the stairs, just looking at me with a sad or longing expression. The first time he awoke in the morning and tried to explain it away as a dream, but after it happened again, he wasn't so sure. Unfortunately, his bladder didn't give him the chance to visit, and when he came out of the bathroom she was gone.

He awoke on more than one occasion to the sound of someone walking on the stairs. He once woke up with a hand on his shoulder, which was a bit startling, but he turned and no one was there.

One night, again responding to the call of nature, he was standing at the commode when a large crash -- like the sound of a chair being thrown onto the wood floors -- made him jump out of my skin. There was a simultaneous vibration under his feet. He checked the whole house to find an explanation, but nothing. Sometimes the old radiators knock, but this was too much. He even checked a website to see if they had had an earthquake, but again, nothing.

At this point he thought, okay, this really isn't necessary, so the next night, awaking like usual in the predawn hours, he got up and headed for the bathroom. He did my business and then decided he and the ghost should have a little talk. He felt like he'd gone insane, but he was compelled to speak aloud to the ghost, which he did.

Standing in his boxers, he apologized for invading her space, and also joked with her about the fact that he was usually in a state of partial or complete undress when walking to the bathroom in the wee hours. He explained that it was a big house, and if she didn't appreciate it she was welcome to turn away or move to another part of the house. He also said that he was not personally concerned about my privacy, but that it seemed unnecessary for her to be floating around when he was doing what men do at the toilet. At any rate, he said, there's certainly no reason to try to scare him, and they should learn to coexist in peace. That was the end of ghostly experiences for him, at least as far as she is concerned.

Kevin said that they don't usually tell their guests about the ghosts unless they ask. Interestingly, their very first guest, when they first opened asked if the house was haunted. A friend of a local writer came once to assess the house. She claimed there were at least seven entities residing here. There were children on the top floor, two stair walkers, something in the dining room, and a guy named Hector who likes to smoke cherry tobacco in the library (numerous people, including Kevin, himself, have smelled the smoke). She also claimed there was "something not human" in the Chestnut Suite. She said that though there are some mischievous energies in the house, she sensed nothing malevolent.

This would be consistent with other's experiences. Some have stated that a presence was at the foot of the bed. One guest stated that someone was sitting on the foot of the bed when she awoke in the morning. At first she thought it was her husband, but then realized he was asleep beside her. There is also a new photograph from a reception they hosted. Distinct orbs are floating throughout the room. This is the only photo in the series with these unexplained balls of light.

There is one spot in the house where numerous independent sources have "felt something." It has been described as an energy. Some feel nothing while others sense that it pushes against them as if to say "Do Not Enter." One friend of theirs was a little disturbed by it, saying that it felt as if he had stepped on a body.

Also, more than one source has stated that the room is occupied by a young woman who would prefer to be left alone. When they rent the room, however, they usually let her know in advance, telling her that she will have a guest, but they won't be staying long. Only one guest complained that she had to sleep with a lamp on because the presence was too strong when the lights were out. Actually, "complained" is too strong a word. After all, she wants to return to spend more time with the spirit.

They've spoken with numerous folks who used to live in the house, and they all had something to say. In general, though, they all say they enjoyed the spirits and loved the house.

Kevin reported that though his wife isn't sensitive to these things (she says she could be surrounded and have no idea), their most recent report from a guest was enough to make her a little nervous about wandering the house alone at night.

Kevin also reported that a guest came down to breakfast one morning and stated, "You have a very busy house." She described a family gathering that went on throughout the night. One man, she claimed, was actually tickling her belly in a playful manner! Kevin's wife showed her some old newspaper clippings about the house that they had found in the local library.

Their guest pointed to a picture of Barney Tarabino and exclaimed, "That's him!" Barney was one of the original homeowners when the house was built between 1903 and 1907.

She said the house was so active that she didn't get much sleep. However, she didn't seem to mind, and she plans to return.

A number of people have asked it they have been able to determine the identities of the various ghosts using local record, however, the above reference to Barney Tarabino is the only direct link they've come across. They have found no history of a Hector (the pipe smoker). The house has changed hands repeatedly over the course of a hundred years, so it's hard to say. As for the nonhuman entities...well.

Two independent sources claim there is some kind of distortion or "wave" that runs through the house. One self-proclaimed expert says he can see the wave when he is standing in front of the house. Interestingly, the location of said wave is consistent with another report.

YAMPA

Yampa is a town in Routt County, Colorado. The population was 443 at the 2000 census.

The Royal Hotel -

Before Kris Ager heard the folklore, she heard the footsteps[26]. When she and her husband, Bill, purchased the historic Royal Hotel about 18 months ago, they knew little about its fabled ghost. But sometimes, experience is the best teacher. Renovation and some restoration began immediately on the interior of the century-old building after the Agers acquired it in August 2000. Kris Ager spent many days sprucing up the guest rooms on the second floor. As she cleaned upstairs one day, Ager said, she heard the sound of footsteps coming down the hall.

The sound echoed more distinctly, she said, because she had not yet placed runners along the wooden floors.

---

[26] 'Haunted' hotel finds new life in Bill and Kris Ager By Danie Harrelson, Staff Reporter to the Steamboat/Pilot Steamboat Today Sunday, January 27, 2002

The footsteps stopped suddenly behind Ager, who said she turned around to find no one there. "It made the hair on the back of my neck stand on end," she said. She thought her husband might be upstairs, she said, but Bill Ager was at work below with a few other men. Kris Ager was the only person upstairs. It was not long after her experience that she learned about the ghost who reportedly makes his home at the Royal Hotel. Rufus has supposedly haunted the hotel since 1918. Stories report he died during a flu epidemic in Yampa when the Royal Hotel provided a makeshift infirmary for patients.

Another tale paints Rufus as a gambler who suffered a fatal gunshot or stab wound after people saw him cheating during a poker game. The playful spirit reportedly pushes furniture, turns lights on and off and flushes toilets. Her supposed run-in with the hotel's oldest resident convinced her of his existence, she said. "I'm not a believer until it happens to me," Kris Ager said. "This made a believer out of me."

The couple continues to work on bringing the historical building back to life, despite the rumors and accounts of occasional visitors. The Royal Hotel, built by Thomas P. Lindsay in 1906, remains noticeably unchanged, despite the effects of time and mishaps on neighboring properties along Yampa's main streets. "It's one of the last buildings that didn't burn down," Bill Ager said. The building requires significant foundational work and the second floor rooms lack any kind of heating system. Both are projects that take time, money and energy — requirements the new owners said they don't mind filling.

The hotel's false front represents the character of buildings in that historical era, said local historian Paul Bonnefield. People in town took advantage of the false fronts to promote Yampa to potential investors, he said. "They used it to make their town appear wealthy," Bonnefield said. Before they purchased the building, Bill Ager said, the land on which it stands might have been worth more than the building. He intends to honor the hotel's original interior as best he can, he said, because the building merits preservation.

People can easily tear down old buildings in the interest of replacing them with something nicer and newer, he said, but so much history is lost in the process. In the meantime, Kris Ager continues to work on refurbishing the upstairs rooms so they can eventually offer guests a small glimpse of the Old West. And she said she'll keep her ears primed, in case Rufus happens to pay her a second visit. "I kind of want to hear them again," she said.

More Ghosts at the Royal Hotel

Frank Powell felt something on the edge of his bed while he was almost asleep one night at the Royal Hotel in Yampa[27]. As soon as he sat up to see what it was, he felt the bed "lift up," as if someone who was sitting there got up.

"I know it sounds like the classic ghost story," said Powell, a Longmont resident, recalling an experience he had while staying at the Royal in 2000. "I didn't see any lights or faces or anything, but I felt something.

"It didn't bother me. It was an adrenaline rush more than anything. But nobody told me nothing about no ghosts."

Legend has it the Royal is haunted by a ghost named "Rufus," dating back to 1918. Some say Rufus' room is No. 6, and others say it is room No. 7.

The rooms are right across from each other at the end of the hall, and most reported encounters come from that area.

According to old newspaper articles, some have said Rufus died from a flu epidemic when the hotel was

---

[27] The Royal ghosts of Yampa: Guests report strange encounters in South Routt hotel By Nick Foster, Staff Reporter to the Steamboat Pilot, Sunday, April 27, 2003

used as an infirmary. Others have said gamblers killed him when he was caught cheating in a poker game.

But Powell doesn't think the ghost he encountered was Rufus. He told his buddies it was a woman. Others back that story, too; one woman says the hotel is inhabited by two ghosts -- a man and a woman.

Kathi Vandegriss, of Strasburg, Pa., was staying in the Royal last summer. In her two-month stay there, she heard footsteps and slamming doors a few times, but actually saw the female ghost "several times." Vandegriss described the ghost as "very young and very pretty."

"She was always in a hurry," she said. "It was always strange to me, but I wasn't afraid. I don't talk about it a lot, because most people will think you're crazy. But it doesn't matter what people say to me; I know what I saw."

Though most describe their encounters as non-threatening, others have been deeply frightened.

Powell wasn't upset with the owners for not telling him about the ghost, but a truck driver and his wife who were visiting a few years ago got upset after their supernatural encounter, Royal Hotel owners Kris and Bill Ager said.

The couple had brought a portable television and was using it as a nightlight while they got ready for bed in room No. 6. Suddenly, the Television went off, even though the power was still on.

The husband turned the television back on and, seconds later, it turned off again. The third time was the breaking point. He and his wife packed their things and walked downstairs.

"I'm not into this," the man told Kris Ager. "This isn't cool."

The man and his wife didn't even ask for their money back. They kept walking, got in their truck and drove away.

The hotel's owners have had some unexplainable experiences themselves.

When they purchased the hotel in August 2000, Kris was upstairs caulking the doorway of the mysterious No. 6 when she heard someone coming up the stairs and down the hall toward her. It sounded like cowboy boots on the wooden floors, she said. When the footsteps came right up to her, she turned and looked out the doorway. No one was there.

"It was a weird feeling, to say the least," Kris Ager said. "I used to not believe in ghosts, but ever since then, I'm a believer."

She didn't know it was haunted at the time. A week later, former owner Linda Kelley told her about the ghost.

"Since then, I've stayed in No. 6 to see if anything would happen," Ager said. "I wish it would happen again."

Ager has not had any other experiences with ghosts. Her personal theory is that since Rufus is supposed to be friendly and he scared her, he doesn't want to scare her anymore.

Bill Ager has heard other things that make him believe one of the ghosts had a dog. He has heard the distinctive sound of paws running. Thinking it was his dog he would call and go looking for him, only to discover nothing was there.

Some have tried to see the ghost through séances during the 1960s, Kris Ager said, but Vandegriss said the ghosts only appear to people who are not expecting it.

INDEX

1

11th Ohio Volunteer Cavalry, 187

A

Acadia Ranch, 81
Alhambra Reception and Treatment Center, 82
Alice, 62
Allen, Ruth and Richard, 100
Alps Motel, 197
Ancient Gods, 4
Anderson, Nathan, 22
Angel of Death, 4
Apaches, 76
Arapahoe County, 144, 145
Arizona, 29, 30, 37, 39, 40, 41, 42, 47, 55, 61, 64, 82, 85, 104, 109, 116, 117, 121, 122
    Bisbee, 15, 16, 17, 18, 21, 24, 25, 26
    Casa Grande, 98
    Chandler, 27, 28
    Douglas, 29
    El Frida, 31
    Flagstaff, 33, 36, 37, 38
    Florence, 39, 40, 41
    Globe, 49, 82, 83
    Jerome, 51, 55, 58, 61, 62, 64, 65, 66, 67, 68, 70
    Kingman, 72
    Mesa, 27
    Oatman, 79
    Oracle, 81
    Phoenix, 27, 28, 82, 84, 85, 87
    Prescott, 88, 94
    Tombstone, 18, 38, 95, 96, 98, 100, 101, 102, 103, 104, 106
    Tubac, 75, 77
    Tucson, 114, 115, 116
    Yuma, 124
Arizona Death House,, 41
Arizona State Hospital, 82
Arizona State Prison, 39
Arizona State Prison Complex–Phoenix, 81
Arizona State Prison's Cellblock 3, 40
Arizona Territory, 17, 36
Army Intelligence Center and School, 41
Army's Information Systems Command, 41

B

Baby Doe, 172, 201
Baldpate Inn, 177
Banters, Jennie, 64, 66
Barrows Boarding House, 104
Barrows house, 103
Beaumont Hotel, 203
Bemis Brother Bag Company,, 156
Bemis Hall, 156, 157
Bergen, Thomas, 182
Best Gals' Room, 123
Best Western Lookout Lodge, 107
Big Bertha's Room, 124
Big Thompson River, 176
Billingtin House, 83
Black Forest Inn, 138
Blackburn house, 103
Brewery Gulch, 16, 17, 24, 26
Broadmoor Hotel, 138

Brook Forest Inn, 182, 183
Brown Palace Hotel, 147
Buffalo Soldiers, 41
Buford House Bed and Breakfast, 95, 100
Buford, George, 95
Butch Cassidy, 198
Byr, Abigail, 91, 92

C

California, 42
California Gulch, 194, 199
Calumet and Arizona Company Smelter, 29
Camp Collins, 187
Camp Hale, 196
Carleton House, 42
Cashman, Nellie, 100
Castle Rock, 20
Chandler High School, 27
Chandler Ranch, 27
Chandler, Alexander John Dr., 27
Cherub statue, 65
Chihuahua Hill, 26
Clanton, Billy, 104
Clantons, 100
Clawson House Inn, 24
Cleopatra Hill, 51
Cleveholm Manor, 208
Clinksdale building, 66
Cochise County Jail., 24
Cogswell Theatre at Colorado College, 156
College Inn, 131
Collins, Victoria, 102
Colorado, 126, 127, 130, 131, 133, 134, 137, 138, 139, 140, 141, 144, 145, 146, 151, 155, 156, 157, 158, 159, 169, 171, 172, 175, 176, 183, 184, 185, 186, 189, 190, 191, 192, 193, 195, 198, 207, 208, 210, 211, 212, 218
Animas City, 173

Aspen, 126
Auraria, 143, 144
Aurora, 131
Berthoud, 175
Black Forest, 138
Black Hawk, 127
Blackhawk, 128, 129, 135
Boulder, 130, 131, 146
Canon City, 132, 133
Central City, 127, 128, 134, 135, 136
Colorado Springs, 156, 158, 159
Cripple Creek, 133, 138, 140, 141
Denver, 131, 133, 134, 136, 137, 142, 143, 144, 145, 146, 147, 150, 152, 160, 162, 164, 165, 168, 169, 172, 175, 182, 199, 200, 201, 202, 212
Denver City, 143, 144
Durango, 173, 209
Empire, 146, 161, 175
Estes Park, 176
Evergreen, 182
Fairplay, 183, 185
Florence, 186
Fort Collins, 187, 188
Glenwood Springs, 188, 189, 190, 193, 201
Golden, 128
Lakewood, 146, 163
Leadville, 172, 194, 195, 196, 197, 198, 200
Longmont, 222
Montana City, 142, 143
Montrose, 209
Ouray, 202, 203, 205
Park City, 184
Penrose, 138
Pueblo, 207
Redstone, 205, 206, 207, 208
Silvercliff, 133
Silverton, 208, 209

St. Charles, 143
St. Elmo, 203, 205
Sterling, 210
Trinidad, 210, 211, 212
Colorado College, 156, 157
Colorado Fuel and Iron Company, 207
Colorado Springs Day Nursery, 156, 158
Connor Hotel, 51, 55
Copper Queen Hotel, 16, 18
Copper Queen Mining Company, 17
Copper Queen Saloon, 17
Crystal River Railroad, 207

D

Davis, George, 97, 98
Days Inn, 35
Days Inn-Airport, 139
Delaware Hotel, 198, 200, 201
Denver and Rio Grande Railroad, 172, 199
Diamond Jack Alterie, 192
Dillinger, John, 114, 115
Doc Holliday, 189, 190, 193
Douglas Reduction Works, 29
Dragoon Mountains, 107
Durlin Hotel. *See* Oatman Hotel

E

Earp
  Wyatt, 100
Earp, Wyatt, 38
Edmunds, Cleopatra "Pietra", 98
Edmunds, Eugene, 98
El Tovar Hotel, 50
Estes, Joel, 176

F

Face on the Barroom Floor, 136
Fairplay Hotel, 185

Fine Arts Center, 156, 158
Flamenco Mental Health Center, 82
Florence Hotel, 186
Fort Huachuca, 41
Fred Harvey Company, 50
Front Range Urban Corridor, 131

G

Gable, Clark, 78
Gadsden Hotel, 30
Gadsden Purchase, 25, 30
Garden of the Gods, 137
Gary Cooper Room, 35
Geronimo, 41
Ghost City Inn, 58
Ghosts of Tombstone, 106
Gilpin County, 127
Gilpin Hotel & Casino, 128
Globe High School, 49
Gold Room, 106
Grand Canyon, 104
Grand Imperial Hotel, 209
Grandma room, 23
Grandmother Garcia, 59
Green Room, 105
Grille Building, 66
Grosvenor Arms Apartments, 150, 151
Guevavi, 73

H

Hand Hotel, 185, 186
Harvey Girl, 50
Harvey, Claude, 56
Harvey, Fred, 50
Hassayampa Inn, 88
Haunted Hamburger, 60
Heart Room, 65
Hearthstone Inn, 139, 155, 156, 158, 159
Hearthstone Inn on Cascade Boulevard, 139

Helshire Inn, 187
Holiday Inn Holidome, 188
Holst, John, 122, 123
Home Rule, 127
Hopi House, 50
Hotel Brunswick, 71
Hotel Colorado, 189, 190, 191, 192, 193
Hotel Congress, 114, 115
Hotel Jerome, 127
Hotel La More/The Bisbee Inn, 25
Hotel Lee, 124, 125
Hotel Monte Vista, 33
Hotel San Marcos, 27
Hotel Vendome, 91
Hotel Weatherford, 37, 38

I

Imperial Hotel & Casino, 142
Inn at Jerome, 63

J

Jarvis Suites, 173, 174
Jefferson County, 182
Jefferson Territory, 182
Jenson, Leone, 85
Jerome Grande Hotel, 55
Jerome Grill, 69

K

King, Stephen, 176, 177, 178
Kiss And Tell Room, 65

L

Ladd, Alan, 34
Lady in Red, 52
Lamplight Room Restaurant, 103
Lariat and Lace Room, 63
Larimer County, 176
Little London, 137
Lombard, Carole, 78, 79

Los Santos Angeles de Guevavi. *See* San Gabriel de Guevavi
Lowell, Miss Julia, 20
Lumber Baron Inn, 132, 160, 161, 164, 165, 166, 167, 168
Lynx Creek Farm Bed & Breakfast, 94

M

Maricopa County, 82
Maricopa Residence Hall, 109
Matchless Mine, 172, 201
Maude's, 58
McCright, W. D., 72
Merryman's Mortuary, 85
Mora, Longino, 121, 123
Murphy's Romance, 40

N

New Mexico, 77, 121, 212
Nichols, Audrey Jean, 30
Noftsger Hill Inn, 49
Noftsger Hill School. *See* Noftsger Hill Inn
North Morton Hall, 36
Northern Arizona Normal School (NANS). *See* Northern Arizona University
Northern Exposure Room, 59

O

O.K. Corral, 102, 104
Oatie, 80
Oatman Hotel, 78
OK Trail, 26
Old Bisbee Bed and Breakfast, 15
Old Company Clinic, 51
Old Episcopal Church, 51
Old Western Hotel, 205
Oliver House, 21
Omega Press, 3
Overland Trail, 187

Oxford Hotel, 169

P

Palace Hotel & Casino, 142
Palmer Divide, 137
Palmer, William General, 137
Penrose, Spencer, 138
Phelps Dodge, 17
Phelps-Dodge Corporation Douglas Reduction Works, 29
Pike's Peak, 127
Pima Indians, 73
Pinal Mountain Juvenile Institution, 83
Pioneer International Hotel, 116
Plum room, 23
Pointe Hilton Tapatio Cliffs Resort, 87
Pratt Bed and Breakfast, 175
Purple Sage room, 23

R

Radisson Hotel, 119
Ramada Inn, 210
Red Garter Bed and Bakery, 120, 122
Redstone Inn, 206
Rochester Hotel, 174
Rock Ledge Ranch, 140
Rocky Mountain National Park, 176
Rocky Mountain News, 169
Rocky Mountains, 203
Route 66, 79
Royal Hotel, 219, 220, 221, 223
Ruby of the Rockies. *See* Colorado, Redstone

S

San Carlos Hotel, 84, 85
San Gabriel de Guevavi, 73
San Juan Mountains, 208

San Marcos Hotel, 28
San Miguel. *See* San Gabriel de Guevavi
San Rafael. *See* San Gabriel de Guevavi
Sara, 31
Sherman Silver Purchase Act, 196
Smith, Soapy, 144
Sonora, 29, 117
  Agua Prieta, 29
South Platte River, 143, 184
Spooks, Ghosts and Goblins" room, 64
St. Cloud Hotel, 133, 134
St. Elmo Hotel, 203, 205
Stanley Hotel, 176, 177, 178, 181
Stone Saloon. *See* Connor Hotel
Stone, Fred, 99
Strater Hotel, 173
Surgeon's House Bed and Breakfast, 61

T

Tabor Opera House, 195
Tabor, Baby Doe, 201
Taft, William Howard President, 193
Tarabino Inn, 211, 213
Tasmania Room, 21
Taylor Hall, 156, 158
Taylor Museum, 156, 158
Teller House, 135, 136
Tenth Cavalry, 41
Tetzlaff, August, 120
Texas
  El Paso, 3, 4, 5
The Ghost City. *See* Arizona, Jerome
Theater Room Museum, 79
Tombstone Boarding House, 103
Tombstone Canyon Road, 15
Tombstone Rose, 103
Trail Ridge Road, 176

U

Unidentified Flying Objects, 6
United Verde Copper Company, 61
United Verde Hospital. *See* Jerome Grande Hotel
University of Arizona, 109
Unsinkable Molly Brown, 192, 198
Utes, 202

V

Verde View Room, 59
Victorian Garden's Bed and Breakfast, 101
Victorian Rose Room, 65, 69
Villa, Pancho, 31, 41
Vision Quest Learning Center, 32

W

Wang. Connie, 4
Wayne, John, 24, 35, 73, 74, 95
White Room, 104
Williams Air Force Base, 27
Windsor Hotel, 171
Wingfield family, 73
Wingfield, Ralph, 73, 74, 77
Wykoff Apartments. *See* Haunted Hamburger
Wyoming
 Fort Laramie, 187

Y

Yampa, 218, 220, 221

Z

Zane Grey Ballroom, 38
Zane Grey Suite, 34

www.ingramcontent.com/pod-product-compliance
Lightning Source LLC
Chambersburg PA
CBHW071609080526
44588CB00010B/1068